$N_o{}^{b}ody's$ R_ib

Nobody's Rib

Pat Stevens,
Liz Sweeney,
Babette, and
Some Other
Women You
Know

NORA DUNN

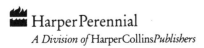 HarperPerennial
A Division of HarperCollins*Publishers*

Photograph credits: pp. 6, 38, 49, 126, Suzy Drasnin/NBC Productions; pp. 33, 34, 36, 58, 76, © Isaiah Wyner/NBC Productions; p. 40, © Norman Ng for Edie Baskin/NBC Productions; p. 42, © Richard Reed for Edie Baskin/NBC Productions; p. 152, Sissi Stein Schneider/NBC Productions. All other photographs are from the author's collection.

FIRST EDITION

Designed by Cassandra J. Pappas

Library of Congress Cataloging-in-Publication Data

Dunn, Nora, 1952–
    Nobody's rib : Pat Stevens, Liz Sweeney, Babette, and some other women you know / by Nora Dunn. — 1st HarperPerennial ed.
      p. cm.
    ISBN 0-06-096498-7 (pbk.)
    1. Saturday night live (Television program) 2. American wit and humor. I. Title.
PN1992.77.S273D86   1991
791.45′72—dc20   90-56425

---

91 92 93 94 95 AC/RRD 10 9 8 7 6 5 4 3 2 1

This book is for
Sarah Glassman
and the rest of the girls

For their support of the work through grief and joy
the author wishes to thank:

> Anne Brody, Kelly Christy, Tom Radtke,
> Anne Macey, Karen Kuehn, Craig Nelson,
> Jeannette Schwaba, Cindy Caponera, Janet
> Capron, Steve Levine, Lorne Michaels,
> Suzanne Gluck.

She wishes to express special gratitude to:

> her father, John, for the poetry
> her mother, Margaret, for the ribs
> and her husband, Ray Hutcherson,
>   for the faith.

CONTENTS

CONTENTS

FOREWORD

After leaving *Saturday Night Live* and finishing this book, I began work on a one-woman show based on some of the characters and pieces in it. I previewed the show in San Francisco and was meanwhile reunited with some of my old friends from the Bay Area. Some of these women that I know, and some that I met during my stay here, are artists who have "broken through," and so we share a common ground, an understanding. One has just published her fourth novel and has had a baby; one is a syndicated cartoonist—the first woman hired by King Features in forty years; one is a journalist; and one is a poet and human rights activist. They are all feminists. Their voices are compelling, funny, intelligent, delicate, angry, compassionate, and playful. They inspire and encourage me, not only by what they say, but because they have carved their own way. They have not compromised their integrity. They have learned to "cultivate around the void," as the Reverend Cecil Williams puts it, and get the work done.

At a time when so much created by the entertainment industry is offensive and dehumanizing, and when I have found myself disillusioned by it, or disappointed in my own work, their voices have come to the rescue. They have drawn me in, comforted me, and challenged me again. I am deeply grateful. I am blessed. I am humbled in the presence of such elegance. Your voices keep me alive.

NORA DUNN
Los Angeles
June 5, 1991

The Beat
According to
Pat Stevens

When I was seven years old my mommy took me to the Amish country. For miles there were fields of wheat and corn and windmills. Miles and miles of tranquil farmland. In short, there was nothing. No vibrant colors, no big bold stripes, no splashy prints. Absolutely nothing. The rich smell of the earth made me sick with despair and I remember getting some of it on my pink bike with the white wicker basket.

I wore red spool-heeled shoes and white anklets with tiny lace trim. In my bright red skort and my matching red ruffled top I was a scarlet vision! Gathered on the street were dark clusters of Amish children. They were different from anyone I'd ever seen before; really odd, just weird. I mean, the outfits. Bleak. Blacks and blues. The boys in brimmed hats and the girls in bonnets. A real throwback to another era. The Depression? It was pathetic. And their faces . . .

Their faces haunt me to this day. They were haunting, haunted faces, like haunted houses. I was so moved I cried. Real tears. Drops.

"Mommy," I pleaded, "Get me out of here!"

I hopped on my little pink bike and tried to pedal away but my training wheels got stuck in, well what else can I call it? Horse duty. It was a nightmare.

Mom said, "Patty, I hope you learned a lesson today."

Oh, I did, believe you me. Since that day I have dedicated my life to those little girls and boys. Mostly the girls. My charm school was a testament to that. The suffering those children were forced to endure—and may still be enduring, I don't know. I don't know a thing about the Amish nowadays, whether they exist or what. If they do I hope they've at least got a Gap now.

Since that experience I have had a recurring dream that continues to this day. It's about a little Amish girl. She's standing a distance away on the side of a road. She peers at me from behind her antique bonnet. I cannot see her figure because she's wearing one of those baggy dresses, but when I look at her feet she appears to be wearing an animal-patterned pump. The sight of the shoes makes me giddy.

4

"Pat Stevens," she calls to me. "Help me, Pat . . ."

Her voice sounds like she needs a glass of sparkling water.

"What can I do?" I call back.

"Help me . . . please! I want to be a model."

With outstretched arms I run to her, but before I get there a horse-drawn buggy driven by a wild, bearded man mows her down. When the buggy is gone all that is left of her is a pair of zebra-striped heels, the kind Manolo Blahnik was showing two seasons ago.

I wake up in a cold sweat, grab a Perrier from the fridge, and pig out on a peach. Always the same pattern. But the face of the little Amish-would-be-model will not go away. She looks a little like Twiggy. Was it Twiggy? But Twiggy wasn't Amish, was she? I thought she was English. Where is Twiggy now?

These questions haunt me still . . .

I am a voracious reader. My favorite book is *Vogue.* Month after month, year after year, I gobble up each volume. I like to think of my head as a big empty bucket, waiting to be filled with pictures, and some

words. Big bold ones. LEGS SILK SEQUINS. I save all my *Vogues*. (I have a *Vogue* library in Canton, Ohio. Come see us!) You should save your *Vogues*, too. What were you thinking last October? Reach for your *Vogue* and it's all there. This way you don't actually have to store anything.

You can leaf through your *Vogue* at your leisure, knowing that another volume is due out in a month. You can linger over a gold woven ankle bracelet, or scurry past an aging face. I do. Once they printed a picture of Georgia O'Keeffe that must have been snapped in the morning before she had her coffee. Golly, that lady got old.

There's so much to see in *Vogue* you may not be able to get to all of it in thirty days. Lots of faces, colors (black skin is in!), noses of all sizes. Look at Paloma Picasso. She makes marvelous accessories, proof that even those of us with deformities, however major, can still do something with our lives. Or with leather or precious stones. Paloma walks that thin line that borders on artsy. BRAVO PALO!

Spend at least one whole day with your *Vogue*. Mill over an article on fitness, then learn new stuff about food . . . "lemon is too assertive with fresh crab." And you'll find it is! My, I love to read. I adore it! Don't be excessive, however. Too much of anything usually shows up on the skin. I shouldn't even be writing so much. We ought to leave that to the masters; van Gogh, Michelangelo, Capezio . . . But leave the thank-you notes and invitations to us, please!

THE BIG BOLD WORDS

Style

Style is contrast: Firm, man-made breasts with a soft, cashmere cardigan.

—Pat Stevens

Long and leggy has met the big buxom blond. A very petite, small-breasted friend of mine asked, "Pat, where do I fit in?" "You don't," I said. I haven't called her since. Style can be a fickle friend. But even if you're small and flat, there still can be something for you. I'm at a loss for what, but something. We're all unique, and those of us who are out of style may come back. So don't mope, cope!

Fur

Fur Is Murder (to Clean)
— PAT STEVEN'S BUMPER STICKER

Come on, don't be a spoily sport. Everybody wants a fur coat. Those who harp about the killing of these positively magnificent creatures are just bitter because they can't afford one (and I can't help that!). I own nine furs—count 'em. And I ain't finished yet, pardon my French! I've got a mink and a lynx and a silver fox, even a leopard. I got that before the big flap about it. It's only been in the last couple of years that I've been able to walk it on Madison Avenue. Can you imagine? I was speaking at a luncheon in Des Moines not too long ago and a gal raised her hand, one of those kooks that call themselves protesters. She said, "Pat Stevens, don't you have a conscience?" I said, "No, I have a chinchilla!" I mean really. . . . You've always got to be prepared with a comeback for these nitwits, apparently even in parts of Iowa! Once one of these nuts accosted me while I was walking my leopard just outside the Diamond Bell Ranch in Tucson, Arizona. Her face was a mass of anger lines. "That animal you're wearing is endangered!" she yelled. I said, "No it's not, it's dead."

Children

*Nothing looks better with a fur than a
bare-bottomed baby.*

—Pat Stevens

I love the word *children,* don't you? Children are
back and making a stronger fashion statement than
ever before. I was having lunch with a dear, dear
friend of mine and we got to talking about her little
girl, Arugula. (Three years old and already looks
better in a bikini than I do—I hate her!) Anyway, I
said, "Cilantro, give her everything. Push her to be
happy, if not ecstatic. Handle her with fur-trimmed
kid gloves. Don't forget, children are our nation's
most precious accessories."

Well, Cilantro looked at me across her cold
pasta salad, eyes misting, and said—well, I don't
remember what she said; it couldn't have been that
important. But we bonded. We're inseparable
friends. She's wool, I'm cashmere; put us together
with a glen plaid and you've got a suit you can take
anywhere.

Lunch

(*see* Children)

Food

Food, we love you, but leave us alone!
—Pat Stevens

Food is back, great big gobs of it. Bulimia, anorexia, schizophrenia—they're all out. Order up heaps of mashed potatoes, red meats, bread with butter, biscuits and gravy. There's nothing more appealing than a gorgeous, thin, full-breasted gal sitting in front of a plate of FOOD. But notice that she doesn't eat it. She pushes it around on the plate. (It's not pushing *her* around!) When you can set a thick slice of pot roast accompanied by boiled potato and roasted vegetable in front of you, then get up and walk away from it untouched, you've won. Food doesn't boss you around anymore. Who said being strong isn't feminine? Hooey!

There does comes a time when I need to let it all go. A time when I've got to get away from everything. Life's harried bustle, the pressures of "The Pat Stevens Show," my horoscope. That's when I pack a few things in my trunks and take off for my getaway condo on Saint Croix. There I can sit out on my veranda (a kind of porch) and drink in the incredible vista before me. The azure blue Caribbean . . . flat and empty . . . it reminds me of my life. The tranquil waters lull me into deep thought . . . I ought to take a swim, it's like bathwater out there. Did I bring my Kamali beach robe? It is only then that the world is mine. Oh, I know there's hunger in it, and famine and war and strife and other bad things, but I love shoes.

THE PAT STEVENS
RANCHO SPA

Yes, indeed, there are haunting questions. Many were asked in the eighties, yet went unanswered. At the Pat Stevens Rancho Spa in Diamond Bell, Arizona, guest speakers raise important questions. While you wallow in a stye of volcanic ash, you can listen to our seminars on convenient portable headphones simply by choosing the channel of your choice.

> Channel 1. Are deep convictions really
>   vitamin deficiencies? Come on, *think*
>   about it! PMS Expert Ralph Snow
>   speaks out.

Channel 2. Are homeless people repaying a cosmic debt? Well, there's got to be *some* explanation! Maybe it *is* in the stars. Dr. Maurice Kelp offers insights into the cosmos.

Channel 3. If *Art* is really a reflection and comment on social conditions, shouldn't it be taxed and not funded? Radio hostess Penny Carter sets us straight on artists who freeload.

Channel 4. Are weird dreams subconscious clues to the psychic interior, or a chemical reaction to deep-dish pizza? Emilia Skelton explores the importance of the low-fat diet. Offers dynamite look-good recipes!

Channel 5. Choosing a Baby: Look Out for the Lemon. Babies are expensive, especially if you want a good one! Author Neal Spinks candidly chatters about choosing your child.

Channel 6. Georgia O'Keeffe: Is Her Biological Clock Still Ticking? Flora Balderston shares her favorite anecdotes about the late artist.

Channel 7. Small Crime and
Punishment: Is *Any* Theft Petty?
Emerson Musk discusses shoplifting,
purse snatching, and the decline of
social values.

Channel 8. Affirmative Action and
Cellulite: One Woman's Heroic Story.
I, Pat herself, talk about my personal
battle with upper thigh fat, and how
I beat it into remission.

Other Questions We Deal With

Who were the boat people?
What is fusilli?
Why is a swatch of fur around a boot
okay, but a coat a crime?
Body fat and global warming: Is there a
connection?
Why clouds?
When did the mug crowd out the cup
and saucer?

There are so many more . . .

DISCOVERING THE
BEAT GENERATION

*T*his fall I went to Chicago to shop at Bloomingdale's. It was magnificent. The whole complex reminds me of Dallas. A delightful blend of chrome and marble like so many upscale malls.

After my shopping spree—if you call buying a couple of pairs of Fogals and a hand and nail cream by Clarins a spree—I went to what I thought was an upscale zoo. There were two magnificent lions in front of the place (not real, of course). So, imagine my surprise when it turned out to be an art museum. And I loved it! No words, just big colorful pictures. While gazing at a Cézanne of a woman gazing at a goldfish in a bowl (how often I have done that, for hours) a young man approached me. Young *and* good looking—Cézanne's painting could not compare to this face and body!

We talked about the painting and I felt my knees shake, this was a deep discussion. I was in over my head immediately. Well, after an espresso in the art museum's cafe, he invited me to a Poetry Slam. No, I'm not kidding. Well, I was as giddy as a schoolgirl, and I must have been temporarily out of my mind, but I accepted, and met him the next night at a club called The Green Mill. Oh, what a place! Cowabunga, as they say!

We sat in a little romantic booth and listened to people, men *and* women, read poems. Some of the poems were good—they rhymed. Others were just all over the place. The master poet of ceremonies actually scared me with his fiery passion.

Well, golly forgive me, I stayed with Elliot for three days in his tiny apartment in Uptown. What a neighborhood of litterbugs! At the time I didn't care, I was blind. I was writing beat poems! By the way, the word *beat* comes from a generation of poets who lived in the fifties. I had no idea those were such bizarre times.

I finally got to a pay phone and called Dr. La Barney, my psychiatrist in New York. He said,

"Pat, this dabbling isn't good for your mind; you might not be able to retrieve it. You're having what's called a brain blowout due to stress and pressure."

And I thought it was just a fling!

Well, I grabbed a cab and took it to the nearest pharmacy. I rushed to the magazine section, and there it was. November *Vogue,* as thick as *Ulysses.* I bought two, and headed for Lincoln Park and the lake. There, sitting on a park bench, I leafed through the pages until a calm fell over me, until I felt the real me coming back. A gentle breeze blew across my face, a damp salty mist off the lake. My God! It suddenly occurred to me I wasn't wearing a moisturizer! Later I was told the lake water *isn't* salty, but at the time . . .

I whisked myself back to Bloomie's, and this time had a much better spree. Bought the whole Shiseido line, deep-pore cleanser, rich facial moisturizing lotion, softening lotion, tonic, eye creme, body creme . . . Most of the morning was over, so I went up to the beauty clinic and bought a half-day of beauty; seaweed body wrap, massage, facial. Suddenly I cried out, "Hello, everybody, I'm Pat Stevens!"

Luckily, no one took notice.

Outside my hotel room at the Ritz I reached into my purse for the key, and found the following poems in it. They are the only tangible evidence of those strange and troubled few days. They are deep expressions from my opened pores, scrubbed, cleaned, and moisturized. A tonic applied to the soul . . .

Imelda, We Hardly Knew Ya

I remember
how deeply she grieves
from inside her
puffy sleeves
her eyes are puffy too
well wouldn't
you
cry
I mean
why
did they have
to keep her
shoes?
That was wrong
they belong to her.
No wonder she

sings the blues.
At least
she looks
best
in that color.

Ivana Wanna Be

The headlines
came crashing down
today.
The Don
cast you away.
Why
Why
Why
The question still
will
not answer itself
as I look down at my scale
I think about my marriage
why
why
why
did it fail?

and the scale
doesn't answer me.

Ivana II

Ivana
you've still got class
and clout
you
work out
you look like Olivia Newton-
John
For Christ Sake!
You've still got pizzazz!
and an accent from where
I don't care!
This is America
land of the free
for all
how tall
are you?

Marla Mapplethorpe

The Don
deserved a brand-new
start

with Marla Mapplethorpe
that big blonde beautiful
work of art.
Marla marla marla
Mapple mapple thorpe
You have no excuses
no abuses
You don't want a billion bucks
like Ivana does
That
Ungrateful
Old
Woman.
Step aside, Ivana.
Lay down in
green pastures
last year's
item.
Give up, please.
Find a new place
for your new face.
This Georgia Peach
looks better on
the
beach
than you do.

Jackie Is Sixty I Can't Believe It

Jackie O, Jackie Onassis
Jackie O Jackie O, Oh
Jackie Kennedy
Jackie Rose
Up
Jackie
You rose up
You made your fortune
You found Maurice
Or he you
Or you he
whatever will be will be.
Jackie Jack
Jackie Shack
Jackie come back.
Caroline, John-John
Baby Rose
Blow her nose
There she goes
she's walking now, Jackie O.
Jackie,
You live in the now
somehow
Art, Culture

A beaded evening bag
never an old bag
or an old hag
Jackie will never let us down
I wish she could wear a crown
On Martha's Vineyard
Or a pillbox hat.

But what's
not
is not
I've said goodbye
to Camelot.
I won't cry
don't die
Jackie
Oh
Jackie don't die
please.

Halston Hello

There will be no
photo
of Halston and me
In *Fame*,
in *Bazaar*
in *Vanity Fair*.

NORA DUNN

No it isn't fair.
Because I was there
too.
But you didn't know,
did you?

I was there
saying hello
saying nice to meet you
saying loved your last line
at JC Penney.
Saying Halston who?
What's his last name?
He's gorgeous
Is he married?

Those questions haunt me still . . .

Liza! Liz! Bianca!
Pleeeze!
Pose with me!

So desperately
So desperately . . .

Well, hey, for petey sakes
I was an up-and-comer too!
I was a living
Fable

The first talk show hostess to
syndicate on cable.
But you
never
said hello.

No Reason for a Tiara

Lady Di
and Fergie
I
Adore thee.
Had it been up to me
we
never would have
broken away.
Over what?
Some tea?
Someday won't you
share a pot with me?
Oh, but for a touch of class
You know!
Won't you please come on my show?
Oh, that will be the day . . .

We need some royalty!
Not some Nancy

strutting like some queen bee.
Or this Mrs. Bush.
Her legs are so big.
Don't you agree?
This country is going to hell.

BACKSTAGE AT "THE PAT STEVENS SHOW"

World Lady Leaders

Margaret Thatcher

Margaret Thatcher has finally stepped down. I guess it finally sunk in that she is not a member of the royal family. I tried to tell her that when she did my show. Could have fooled me, though—she looked like a horse! (My sources say the Queen lives in utter fear of breaking a leg or an ankle.)

Cory Aquino

Recently Cory wrote telling me she now spells her name with an *i*—Cori—and that she's trying to break into modeling. I told her, forget it, you're old and you have a flat, unphotogenic face. She took it well, though I can't be sure; we communicated through mail only. I told her to get ahold of Ed McMahon. She could be a female spokesperson. (Well, golly, I had to tell her something, the woman was desperate.) Maybe she could do Reebok or Nike, the woman is definitely on the run. And Cori, if you're listening, *get a man.*

Benazir Bhutto

If Beni had listened to me and gone into modeling, she wouldn't have had the trouble she did. She never did the show; she was always too busy. She sets a fine example as a woman who never knew what she could do best. Classic features and she went into politics! It makes me so sad I could grieve.

Jerry Hall

Not a world leader but she ought to be. When Mick married her he became Mr. Hall. Jerry taught me

that if you stand on your head, or turn yourself upside down on a chair, all the blood rushes to your brain. Do this every day and you'll look prettier. I did. I never looked like Jerry does, but I found that when I stood up again, I could *think*. What a rush!

Jimmy Breslin

Okay, he's not a lady. He's a humble man, though. Not only did he write a book, the picture on the cover was quite good! A very realistic rendition. But he simply wouldn't take credit. He'd won a Pulitzer Prize for writing, but for my money, he should have won for his drawing. Now that I'm writing I can see it's not that hard, just time consuming. But I can't draw a cat! That takes talent.

Barbara Bush, Kitty Dukakis, and Elizabeth Dole

I don't know what can be done about Barbara. Probably nothing now. Couldn't she at least go to salt and pepper? And by gosh, I found out she wasn't the President's mother right on the show! I covered very well, I thought, simply by saying it wasn't my fault—my god, look at her! But this was so long ago

and she turned out to be nice and sort of athletic. Kitty is another story. Kitty, stop talking about booze! You make me crave gin. Warm. Out of the bottle. I take a nip now and then, but I'm not writing about it, except in this sentence. (A husband as understanding as Michael would drive me to drink nail polish remover too!) I rooted all the way for Elizabeth Dole. So pretty and stylish and smart. (Read her book!) I voted for her and Dan Quayle. I mean, golly, wouldn't it be nice to have two good-looking people in the White House? Not that I don't stand behind my President, just as the wives do, but he's got to make some decisions on hair color, too. I mean, his hair isn't any particular color. I wonder if he knows who Bill Forsythe is? (I'll bet Reagan did.) Bill's hair is white and dashing, like Barbara's. Mr. President, go silver or something.

Missy Stevens

My daughter's not a world lady leader and she never will be. I can't believe she's even part of me, she's so less than perfect. And I've been supportive! Having my daughter was the biggest mistake of my life. Instead of learning my lesson, I had her on my show. (Not the birth—I mean thirteen years later). I don't know if any of you have had a baby, but it's

NORA DUNN

38

like giving birth to an alien. Dr. La Barney says we never bonded. Well, how was that supposed to happen? I had to spend the first year in the gym! Was I supposed to breast-feed on the Stairmaster? Actually, in those days we didn't even have Stairmasters—part of the tragedy. While I was sweating it out on a stationary bike trying to get my thighs back, Missy was lollygagging in a sandbox somewhere with her Jamaican nanny, not a care in the world. And that's what life was like with Missy: me working and her playing. I literally had to drag her to commercial auditions. She's got talent somewhere, and for a while I had the patience to dig for it. But no more. She lives with Dad now. Am I bitter? A little. Someday she'll pay me back for all my hard work, probably with a book. Missy, Mommy still loves you, even though your posture is atrocious.

Beverly Johnson, Kim Alexis, Cheryl Tiegs, and Herb Lacrue

An experience almost as humiliating as Missy's appearance. Good gosh. I'd given my first modeling clinic at The Pat Stevens Rancho Spa. Beverly Johnson arrived first and I was ecstatic! But then Herb Lacrue, a catalogue model, showed up. A day later Cheryl and Kim arrived, but all Herb did the

Pat Stevens with her daughter, Missy, and Fred Savage.

whole weekend was tell us his troubles and beg to have his picture taken with the girls. Worse thing was, he wanted the photos taken with him in his drawers! He'd been an underwear model. To top it off, he insisted on coming on my show. I said no, but he showed up and some clown miked him. (That clown is working at a different circus now!) Well, Herb couldn't stop talking about himself and his divorce. Finally I snapped. I blew my cool for the first time on television. I said, "Herb, we all have our problems in this life, but we rub in a little Grecian Formula and get on with it." Mouth dropped open, nothin' more to say. I'll always be grateful for those gals, coming to the spa and on "The Pat Stevens Show," but I will never forgive Herb for spoiling my most shining moment. Because of him, I never buy men's underwear and I urge you to do the same. Don't even look at the catalogue pictures. Sometimes you just have to take a stand.

DIARY DEAREST

September 1989

Hurricane Hugo hit Saint Croix. Thank god none of my people were involved in the looting. The damage was devastating, extensive, and heartbreaking. And I don't know what happened to anybody else's place! Mine kept the help too busy to handle their own troubles, thank goodness. What a mess.

Dr. La Barney talked me through many bouts of despair, then turned me on to Saint Bart's. Saint Croix who?! This place is paradise. It reminds me of what the Riviera once was (not the one in Vegas). I bought a shameless string bikini at a darling boutique in Gustavia, definitely not to be worn by a big-boned midwestern gal. As a matter of fact, you don't see her kind here at all. Those kind of people gall me anyway; they just *chew* up the scenery.

Saying good-bye to my Virgin Island staff was painfully sad. In fact, I didn't. I ought to drop them a line sometime.

Christmas Memory, 1989

Xmas shopping in New York. I adore it. I ask myself, Did I buy too much for myself, and not enough for others? That question will always haunt me. As will the bells at Rockefeller Center, chestnuts roasting, the chocolate at Godiva. I step into Saint Patrick's to thank the dear Lord, but it's packed. On to Saks. Before I hit the door, a tattered woman approaches me: the little match girl grown up. She tugs at my heartstrings. I reach in my purse—an alligator clutch, I never carry a shoulder bag and you shouldn't either; eventually it will throw you off kilter. Where was I? My heartstrings . . . I give the poor lady fifty cents. Poverty is such a terrible thing, because there's *nothing* we can do about it.

August 13, 1990

Sometimes while reading *Vogue* it just makes my head spin. When will I learn to stick to the pictures, stick to the pictures. That ought to be my mantra. Don't tell me silk comes from a scalded worm! My great grandmother died of a tapeworm, a very painful memory had I been there. And all this talk of pulp and Africa, viscose and toxic methods. My Lord, am I supposed to run around naked? And now, as if fur weren't enough, leather kills! What am I supposed to do, take it out of my own hide? Today, *Vogue* is a bummer. I must be insane even to think that.

Called Dr. La Barney.

August 13½

Saw Dr. La Barney. Feel smashing. Nothing's my fault.

August 14

New York hot and sticky, but I must shop. Bergdorf's feels cool and comfortable. I spot a whole batch of thigh-high boots studded with decorative

45

baubles and ribbons. Vittadini to Frizon to Laurent—you're crazy! And I love you.

Quick flash of horror—Am I too old for all of this?

Dial up Dr. La Barney from powder room. Brief chat. I'm the one who's crazy for even thinking about the elderly.

1:30 P.M. Lunch at the Plaza with Gloria Von Somebody. Shades of Ivana make me wistful.

2:30 P.M. Back to Bergdorf's for the boots.

August 29

Had session with Dr. La Barney. He fell asleep! I tiptoed out without waking him.

August 29, P.M.

La Barney really peeved with me. Seems he slept through the next three sessions. He's going to charge me for them! The next session we will talk about responsibility.

September 1

Daughter Missy decided to live with her dad forever. La Barney told me to get a cat. So I did, a Persian. Named it Tip Toe!

September 4

Emotional session with Dr. La Barney about my difficulty relating to ribbed knit sweaters. I've got to get over it by late fall. They're a staple item in any winter collection this season.

Woke Dr. La Barney and left. Saved myself three hundred dollars!

September 7

Tip Toe has been a miserable experience. I've done everything for her, but she's worse than Missy. A complete clod. This afternoon she broke my Steuben elephant! I'd like to kill her and make it look like an accident.

October 24

Went for a session with Dr. La Barney. It was gut wrenching. He talked incessantly about his fear of aging. Was very upset when I told him my time was up.

October 25

La Barney out of town for six weeks. He went to have a face-lift in South America. (Now how can he afford that?!) His secretary, Patsy, tells me La Barney saw a special on PBS about this terrific plastic surgeon. The best in the world. Maybe I ought to start watching public television.

October 26

I'm going bonkers without a therapist. La Barney was such great company. Patsy referred me to Dr. Denise Vennetti. A girl! Golly, am I in a pickle . . .

October 27

My pores are getting larger every day. I've got to see a therapist.

Denise Vennetti, Ph.D.

October 28

Vennetti's got the whole day free.

Vennetti's office is full of pictures of herself. Posters actually. Her secretary sits and stares at herself in a vanity mirror.

When I enter Vennetti's office, she's sitting in an easy chair looking at herself in a vanity mirror. Without looking up, she says, "Hello. [then a long pause] Sit, please. What is your problem?"

"First of all," I say, "I'd like it if you'd put down the mirror and look at me."

"You're here to look at yourself," she says, "not to look at me or to comment on me looking at myself."

Then I say to myself, This gal's giving me the heebie-jeebies.

Almost as if she could read my mind she says, "So I give you the heebie-jeebies?"

I must admit I was a bit taken aback, I mean, I didn't think I was going to see a psychic! If she could tear herself away from the mirror, would she pull out a Ouija board?

"Well . . . it's just that I really need a therapist," I said. "You see, Dr. La Barney was a big part of my life. He, well, needed me. . . ."

Vennetti finally looked up from the mirror. "You

don't feel needed? You in fact feel needless, needy, needing. Unwanted. Discarded. Within your need-lessness you feel a sense of betrayal, of emptiness, of despair, despairing, disparaged, ravaged, under-nourished, flushed, snotty, sweaty, and chilled. Sounds like you have a cold. That's okay. It's okay to have these feelings. It's very natural. It's very healthy in the sense that you're acknowledging that you're sick. You should also know that colds are incurable."

I didn't dare think what I wanted to, that she was a sick nutcase wacko. Maybe I could wait it out. Maybe she'd doze off. . . .

"It's natural that you should feel hostility toward me," Vennetti said. "Here. Take the mirror. Take it, it won't bite you. Look into the mirror, at yourself. That's right. Look at yourself. Keep looking. Go on. . . . What do you see? Don't tell me, tell your-self. Who's in there? Look at yourself. Your pores are wide open. Walk through them, look inside your face into your soul. Now put the mirror down. Down! That's right. I want to tell you about my par-akeet, Charlie Sheen. Charlie didn't know he was a bird until I got him a little vanity mirror and put it in his cage. I said, Look Charlie, you're not an actor. You're a bird. Look at yourself. Well, he did. He was depressed for several days, but he kept looking. He stopped just long enough to eat a little seed and have a drink of water. It was very intense therapy he was undergoing. Finally, on day ten, he began to sing again. He crept around on his perch a little. He started to peck away at his treat tree. And that's what will happen to you. You'll rediscover your treat tree. But you have to look. If you don't look at yourself, you'll spend the rest of your life on your perch, gnawing at your cuttlebone, never knowing why, never knowing who you are. Never knowing exactly what a cuttlebone is. . . . Do you know what a cuttlebone is? Never mind. Don't wonder. I can tell that's not your bag. Go. Leave now. Go look at yourself, I'm tired of looking at you. Give me the mirror. Give me the mirror, it belongs to me. Thank you. Go. Get out! Pay the receptionist."

I left Vennetti's office a new woman. Stopped at a pet shop and bought a cockatiel.

December 7

Totally bogged down by Christmas. I miss Missy, but I'd never tell her that. Anytime I say anything affectionate it goes right to her head.

December 8

La Barney returned. Can't wait to see the results. I've been watching PBS, almost unbearable. I flick the channel occasionally to catch a commercial.

December 10

La Barney looks like George Hamilton. (Considering he used to look like Alfred Hitchcock, it's a miracle!) He's a different man, like a whole new therapist. I told him about Vennetti and he charged me a referral fee. Thank God he hasn't changed! He expressed interest in the Vennetti technique, then asked to borrow my compact. Stared at himself the rest of the session.

December 15

Final entry for awhile. Must confront Christmas head on. So many, many gifts to get. All my employees. The biggest challenge is matching the names to the faces. Why don't we just use a piñata? I know what Missy wants. Money. La Barney asked for a good facial moisturizer. And what the heck do you get a cockatiel? It should come to me. This whole business is for the birds!

December 31, 1990

Last entry . . . I long for the eighties, don't you? It seemed every day was a gift, something new. A car, stockings, a fun fur hat. Christmas 1989 was the most exciting, and the most nostalgic. I looked back at all of my shows, all of the guests that graced the chair beside me. I've got a great big scrap book so I don't forget. Who knows what the nineties will bring? I want more more more! More guests, more things. I was in a shopping mall in Chicago last week, I was there for a spring fashion show I did called "Sprinkles of Spring," and I visited Watertower Place. I was riding the escalator, breathing in that wonderful fresh air. Oh, don't shopping malls make you want to live forever? You can't, you know. You can look good for a long time if you have some work done, but we haven't come up with a cream for everlasting life yet. Long after we're gone, however, there will still be talk shows, and cable will be more acceptable. For that, I thank God.

You know, *Vogue* used to be the only book I read, until *Fame* came out, and *Premiere,* and *Smart,* and *Buzz.* Now I have expanded my horizons. And when I've finished gobbling up every word and my big empty bucket is full, I just pour it out and start over!

AN INTERVIEW WITH ACTRESS ASHLY ASHLEY

*T*empestuous, difficult, elusive. Three words that best describe actress Ashly Ashley. Broadway baby to movie maven. Bouts with booze, boyfriends, and a moped accident that left her badly bruised, she's more than a Hollywood survivor. She's its current champion. Writer June Joyce caught up with her in her trailer in Malibu.

JJ: In your opinion, what do you think of the creative state of the art today?

AA: I think—and I do think, I often think, I think thinking plays a key role in the thought process. I

Ashly Ashley with Robert Downey, Jr.

think as far as thought goes, the Industry is in trouble and it's up to the members of the Industry, not just the Academy, to do something about it, or at least to think of doing something about it.

JJ: For instance . . .

AA: How does one create a character? How do I create a character? Me. How do I do it? In order to get to where I want to go, I have to stop the thought process and get creative. That's why I'm in this trailer park now. I don't want to think or be connected to thinking. I've got to peel off the layers and layers and layers and layers of depth that I have to get down to the virgin flesh, that *thing.* And it is a thing, in which we do, which is to say one must do what one's thing is. Or at least think one is doing one's thing. That is what, I think, becomes what the state of the art is. You must *make* what you do a *thing.*

JJ: What do you call this layering process?

AA: The layers and layers and layers and layers of depth? I call that the baklava technique, due to its Greek origins. It was the Greeks, of course, who started all this incredible madness which we now call The Theater. It's exciting!

JJ: And baklava is so rich . . .

AA: One would not want too much.

JJ: What about pain?

AA: It hurts. Somehow hurt is a part of the creative process of an actress. And I think in life, too. That's why it was so painful to write my book, because it's about my marriage and my life from beginning to now. It's called *The Difficult Years* and will come out this Christmas.

JJ: I understand a great deal of it is pictures.

AA: Yes. I remember so many things that way. I'm an actress, an artist. I'm a performer. It's so difficult to explain in words. I know something in an organic way, I think, and I have this tremendous need to pass all that along to the little people. And I don't mean that in a derogatory way. I call them the little people because when I'm up there on the stage looking out at that sea of nameless faces, they really do look tiny. That's what makes people in the theater feel so big. That's what enables us to do this extraordinary thing we do. This gift. When the lights go down and the spotlight hits me, the whole audience disappears. It's magic. Absolutely. I love it!

That fourth wall comes up. Other actors have often stated that when they're on the stage with me, they disappear, too. They don't exist. That's the reward.

JJ: You went through what many people in your field have gone through, didn't you? A period that you perhaps are not proud of.

AA: I did, yes. Drinking. I was looking for answers at the bottom of a bottom. My own. I mean, my work, my acting, became about my bottom. I had a great bottom, especially before I started drinking. And, well, that led to the sex, the drugs, too. I had left the theater and I was making a lot of money doing movies, meeting a lot of men, doing drugs. At the time, it was great, great fun. But now I realize I wasn't happy at all. What felt like so much fun for those years, well I know now, through therapy, and of course The Clinic, that I didn't have any fun.

JJ: That's too bad. Because the public perceived your life then as being fun.

AA: I looked happy, and I felt happy. Well, not happy, euphoric. That's a whole different thing. And my memories of that time are, thank God, very happy ones. I remember it as happy. But it was a false high and I urge young people especially not to do it. If you're older and established and don't have that much to lose, it might be okay. But for those starting out, visualize peace.

JJ: Exactly. You were lucky to be so successful on film and on Broadway. Why did you drop out?

AA: My vision had become so blurred after my success. I had abandoned the theater. My marriage to Dev was over and had ended very badly. It's no secret that I came home one night and he was wearing one of my dresses. I wouldn't have minded except he didn't ask. You can imagine what it was like when it came time to divvy up the goods. I was living in Hollywood. I live in New York, but I was spending most of my time in my house in Beverly Hills. I was a work freak, a control freak, a health food junkie. One day I got out of my pool, slipped and hit my bottom very, very hard. It made a very, very large bruise. There's nothing much you can do about a bruise except wait it out. And you know I had had that moped accident in the Caribbean. That bruise was a painful memory. So I stood there and looked at this bruise for a long time, and of course I could because I've taken a lot of yoga. But it wasn't my bottom that was bruised, it was my soul. I had to *work* again. So I went to Kentucky, a right-to-work state. I had to relearn the creative process. I wanted to do a documentary; I wanted to write pages and pages and pages of prose poetry, do some performance pieces that nobody would *judge.*

JJ: Any contact with the outside world?

AA: No, just *US* magazine. They were with me the whole time. They were my lifeline, so to speak. But I didn't let anyone define my work, and it worked. It was terrific. Nobody discussed it, nobody cared about it, nobody *saw* it. That was disturbing. But then art *is* to disturb. That's the nature of the beast. It comes from the heart and hits you in the gut. *I* define my own work. It's tepid, it's sleek, it's seductive, succinct, lean, stylized, reformed—there's no word for it. *It* is the thing. It *becomes* the thing. The complexities are so complex they're almost microscopic. It's contradictory. It's like sex. It's repulsive yet easy to look at. I work inside a genre, compulsively, from a place that feels good. I twist it until it feels bad, it's painful, then I loosen up on it and let it come again and again and again. Because the product in the long run has to be fun. I mean, we're making entertainment for the masses, for those tiny faces I described from the theater. And it has to work on a popcorn-chewing, visceral level or nobody's going to see it. The experience will dissect because it will not be fun. And that's what I learned from these people in Kentucky. These real people. Over coffee. I mean, we had a dialogue in which I spoke to them and they listened to me and they said, "Fuck you, we don't understand you, get out!" I got that message. Very clearly. It was pure unmasticated hurt they were expressing. That's what got me back to Hollywood. Those people did. God, I love those people in Kentucky.

JJ: You came back and you've made a new movie. What can you tell us about the film?

AA: After my experience in Kentucky I needed a really interesting project and I was ready to do something really, really intense. The film I've just completed, well, it's a terrific project, because I worked with a woman director, a woman wrote it, and it's about a woman. It's called *Cop,* in which I play a character called Buddy who's a tough, ballsy detective. The gun is the sex object in the film, so I was free to be me, to be whoever I am, and that was exciting. It was directed by Jenny Steffenhuer— she's just brilliant. And I was, well, I did my best work to date, and I've done some damn good stuff, so you can imagine. I had to kick ass, I had to sweat, I had to claw, I had to cheat—and that was just to read for the part. To the outsider this business looks like glamour. But you've got to crawl into that sewer, lift that manhole cover and get inside, every day, to stay in the business. It's tremendously rewarding. And the money can be tremendously rewarding. That's the payoff.

JJ: You're so right. Have you seen the film?

AA: Yes. I wept. The film tears your insides out, jumbles them up, rearranges them, and puts them back together again. In that order. It's a disturbing piece. It's violent and the violence is absolutely seductive. It's about a psychotic serial-killer rapist attorney who I kill just as he's being executed in the electric chair. It's a strong statement and it works on three levels. We shot it on location, in L.A., so, it's a gritty piece.

JJ: What's next?

AA: I'm sailing with Greenpeace. I mean, we're burning down the Amazon, we're trashing the planet. We need to listen to the Indians, the ones who are left and who of course are sober. I love the American Indians; they're a tremendous interest to me. I can't just sit by and let Western civilization destroy God, the organic one. Maybe I'm made of more intense stuff than the rest of us. . . . Yes. I am. I know I am . . . I think my career speaks for that. Maybe that's the "Buddy" in me. Art imitates life and so forth. But things are such a mess, you know. Something in me has to save that *thing*. Because it is, of course, a *thing*. And it's important to think of the thing in that way I think. Thinking is part of the process.

TREVOR HELSINKI: SEQUEL TO A PHENOMENON

*H*is directorial debut was a box office tamale. His second effort was even bigger, scorching the summer box offices and raising Tinsel Town's eyebrows higher than the skirts on Sunset Boulevard. Now the Belgian-born filmmaker is Joel Tartar's choice to direct the seventy-million-dollar mega-thriller *Gunload*, set to begin shooting this month. Peter Mintor talked to Trevor Helsinki poolside at his rented digs in Brentwood.

PM: Where did it all begin?

TH: I started making films in Europe. I attended the prestigious Film Institute of Belgium, where I learned film technique and wrote scripts. I made six films there, but my work was not really well received. It was in fact deemed mediocre and childish. They said it had no content and could never appeal to thinking human beings. It was then I knew my dream to be a Hollywood filmmaker could be realized.

PM: What intrigued you about this country?

TH: There was a lot of noise in America, and I was dying to be a part of it. They picked up on that right away in Hollywood, and I worked immediately, directing *Narc Squad III, The Final Chapter.*

PM: Now, who made the first two? I don't recall.

TH: No one. The studio felt the film had a better chance as a sequel, if the audience thought they'd seen the first two. So, we used the trilogy genre. And it worked, to the tune of three hundred million dollars.

PM: Holy mackerel!

TH: Yes, that's a lot of clams! Now all the studios are doing it. Why make the first and second when you can start with the third?

PM: Exactly.

TH: A fan actually told me they thought *Narc III* wasn't as good as *Narc I,* so tell me the audience isn't stupid! The studio gambled on that notion, and they won.

PM: You'll earn ten million dollars for directing Joel Tartar's *Gunload.*

TH: Go for it, right? It's a fairy tale. I love making big action flicks. One hundred million dollars buys an awful lot of magic, doesn't it? I heard that after audiences saw *Narc III,* they stayed in the mall, wandering around aimlessly, sort of in a dream state. It's an interesting phenomenon worth examining I think. These films are very effective, but of course the critics can't see it.

PM: I thought it got two thumbs up.

TH: One up, one down. I still think it's magic.

PM: There are some critics who are really down on your work.

TH: Yes, they say it's junk. And it is! Garbage is the issue of the nineties, and I'm dealing with it. The movie industry is embracing it with zeal, we're wrestling with it, creating it, and we will master it. I'm not worried about that at all. Somewhere in me there's a whale movie, a fur movie, a pollution movie that's going to emerge. That intrigues me too. And it will happen. It's an interesting phenomenon worth examining I think.

PM: But what about the violence? People are saying enough is enough, tell us a story. What's happening to our cultural myths?

TH: I don't read you.

PM: What I mean is, what's happened to romance? If Audrey Hepburn or Donna Reed were acting today, would they be playing hookers and cops? When will women get to play the pimps?

TH: Soon! And they'll be delightful! That's an interesting phenomenon worth examining, I think; one that I feel is worth a closer look. And so is prostitution. Not the nasty kind, certainly not the male kind or anything. I'm talking about the light-hearted kind of prostitution. I explored that territory in an early film about a hooker who wouldn't take any money and who didn't have a pimp. She had a heart of solid gold. It would have been a wonderful role for Donna Reed.

PM: But is there too much killing in your movies?

TH: What's too much? Is one life cheap, but two hundred going too far? We're just having fun. People should lighten up on this thing with violence. You'd think we were using real blood or something, which we aren't. In this day and age it would be too dangerous. And I think it betrays the genre anyway.

PM: What will you do after *Gunload*?

TH: I've always wanted to explore American comic books, that whole phenomenon. When I was little, I would look at the comic-strip pictures hoping they would come to life, but they never did. I had to use my imagination in those days. Now that I'm a filmmaker, I don't have to do that. That's the beauty of it.

PM: Which one will you make?

TH: You're asking a little boy in a candy store, you know. Heh, heh. *Little Lotta* intrigues me. What happened to the fat girl when she grew up? I'd love to see Kim Basinger do it. I want to blow the lid off, you know, that other lid, the one we don't want to look under.

71

PM: And can you see beyond *Little Lotta*?

TH: You're tough, but I like you! You're pushing all my buttons and I need that. I can see some parts of the future, and I'm going to tap into social consciousness, that market. My whole whale, fur, off-shore drilling, air-pollution movie is brewing in there somewhere. I'm a creative stew pot, and somebody, I don't know who, keeps adding another vegetable or lamb shank to me.

PM: What was your favorite film?

TH: Why be modest? *Narc Squad III.* I loved some of my early ones too, the ones I did in film school. I still watch them, usually with a pretty lady. I was exploring sex in those days, which was an interesting phenomenon worth examining then. Female nudity interested me a great deal, how the female form looked when it was giving sex, or having sex, however you see it. Now they just seem like silly skin flicks to me, but I do enjoy them. With the right lady!

Trevor Helsinki threw his head back and laughed a deep, devilish chortle as rich as Belgian chocolate. The tan, sandy-haired man-boy, who lives inside of his action flicks as if they were his private club-house, indeed has an infectious charm, an energy.

He churns over social issues as if his soul were an Osterizer. Suddenly, I was laughing too. My laugh was more like a Snickers bar, but it felt good nonetheless. For one brief shining moment I sat up there with Trevor at the top of the Hollywood Heap, and it felt good. Damn good.

CONFESSIONS
OF A SEX KITTEN

She's Babette, the international sex kitten. Her odyssey to find an identity as a performer and as a woman started in the United States, but led her to France and back. A singer-comedienne, an actress, and an entrepreneur, she talks with Richard Flounder about her life, loves, and ambitions.

RF: You've "done it all," as they say. How would you like to be remembered after the dust settles?

BSK: I'd like to be able to say that I'd really made a mess of my life, that way I would know I lived it to the fullest.

NORA DUNN

RF: You started out in the business at fourteen. Why did you first get up on the stage? You were a singer, weren't you?

BSK: No, no. I was a, how do you say, cake popper. You know, I came out of a cake at parties, I pop out.

RF: How long did that last?

BSK: Until I tore a ligament in my knee and had to have surgery. I fell in love with the physical therapist and lived with him for several years. We had a baby together.

RF: But what drove you to perform?

BSK: The baby did. She was always crying. So I would sing her a little song, louder and louder. It helped me to develop my voice and to find my identity. The truth was I didn't know who I was.

RF: How did you find out?

BSK: Somebody told me. I always had this accent, not like an American, more like a French. And everybody said I looked French. So I flew to Paris alone and it was remarkable. I knew it, I knew Paris like déjà vu. I went to the countryside, to Nice, to Chardonnay, and it all felt very spiritual. Then I went to Saint Tropez, and I was hooked. I knew I was French! And not only was I French, I was Wooman!

RF: You say Wooman. Why?

BSK: Well, the French invented the word *wooman.* It came from the tiny word *man,* which is actually an American word, an Anglo word, and only a small part of the big picture. So we took that little word, and we put the French word *woo* in front of it, and there you have it. Wooman. Woo! Woo! Woo! Woo!

RF: Okay, okay. How did your film career start?

BSK: Well, I met Louis Plappi and he put me in his first film, *And God Created the French,* which was so prophetic for me because I felt I had been reborn. We made six more films together. He was sort of my pimp.

RF: You've always preferred to be called a sex "kitten." Why not "goddess" or "symbol"?

BSK: To me, "goddess" symbolizes ancient myth, and I don't want to be associated with age. And sex symbols, they always die. Like Marilyn Monroe. She was mysterious, and she died mysteriously. Her death remains an unsolved puzzle. We still don't know which one of them killed her. And then Jayne Mansfield, well, her head came off, and she died. But a sex kitten never dies, we just get fluffy.

RF: You made six films with Plappi.

BSK: Yes. Then it went sour and I went to Hollywood. I was so lucky to be a sex kitten and still get strong female leads. My first film was *Female Firefighter, Centerfold U.S.A.* Then I made *Victim with a Vengeance* and *Dead Nurse.* A nurse has a lot of responsibilities. That role was a learning experience and a challenge. I loved the character, the strength. Then she died—she gets murdered. It took a long time for me to get over that.

RF: Is that why you don't want to die?

BSK: No, no. I don't want to die because I like it here so much, I love the beach. But I will face the fluff as it comes.

RF: You now say you want to be taken seriously, yet you just did another spread in *Pinup Bunny.*

BSK: Look I have a good body and I have the right to exploit it. I control it. Just because I expose my derriere and my breasts does not mean I don't have a brain. It's in every picture too, right under my hair—use your imagination for goodness sake!

RF: But you've begun to undertake more serious projects.

BSK: Yes. I'm doing three movies for TV— portraits of wooman in different walks of life. I will make *Portrait of a Showgirl, Portrait of a Female Runaway,* and *Portrait of a Naked Slut on Drugs.* If you want to make female movies in Hollywood, you have to make some compromises.

RF: Can we talk about your most famous affair? You know, the one with the Premier?

BSK: Yes, okay. I dated Leonid Brezhnev. It was big news all over. It was all over the pages of *Pravda.* The public had a misconception about the whole thing. They saw him as cold and withdrawn, and thought I took advantage of that. All wrong. He was a blast. We met at Club Med at an all-you-can-eat salad bar, something they did not have in Russia, and even now under Gorby they still do not. Anyway, Brezhie's plate was so funny. He had loads of Jell-O, large-curd cottage cheese, shredded carrots, macaroni, three-bean salad, beets, beets, and more beets, and garbanzo beans, all smothered in

French dressing and Bac-O bits! I laughed, and he laughed. He said, "How about you help me eat this?" Next thing you know I'm in his room, poolside.

RF: It lasted . . .

BSK: Many weeks. I'm including some of the details in my, how do you say, memoir.

RF: So you *are* writing a memoir?

BSK: Oh, I'm trying, but I can hardly remember a thing. Isn't that a shame? I wish I wrote things down. Most of what I wrote down I wrote in a French accent and I can't read it.

RF: What's the little secret about Brezhnev that you have under your sleeve?

BSK: Well, all right then. Don't tell. His eyebrows, you remember, were big and bushy. It made him have a very commanding presence, he thought. Well, one night we were getting into bed, and he took them off! They were little hamsters. Live! He put them in a little cage next to the bed. He was in pain because of them, clinging so tightly to his face. But he was addicted, you know, afraid he wouldn't be accepted if the Russians knew he had these thin, sharp eyebrows, like Divine. I really felt for those hamsters, clinging to his face for their very lives, because if they fell off—death. They were shot. This is before glasnost, remember. And try eating out, all the time worrying if one would drop off into the soup! Oh, in the end I couldn't live with that. Such a distraction. After we parted he sent me a tiny little hamster pelt jacket for my troll doll—I have a collection. That's the Brezhie I remember and write about.

RF: Truth is stranger than fiction.

BSK: When you travel in international circles it is. And I'm an international sex kitten, you know.

RF: Your next project?

BSK: I'm somewhat of an entrepreneur, you know. I was taking a trip across the country, to see it, you know, to see if I remembered it the way I remembered France. I was driving in my Maserati very fast, trying to get away from Ohio, and suddenly I see this beautiful river. I pulled into a gas station and asked the attendant where I was. We had a brief affair, which resulted in a child, and then I went on to West Virginia and bought the whole state. It's quite lovely. I love the blue mountains.

RF: What will you do with it?

BSK: Absolutely nothing. That's the kind of sex kitten I am. Rustic. Rustic sex kitten!

RF: What about later, really? You say you'll just get fluffy, but you must worry about fading. You've enjoyed the life of a beautiful woman.

BSK: Men always ask that question. They love to see a beautiful woman grow old. It's the only time that they can feel superior to us. Then they speak of us in the past tense. . . . I hope to do it gracefully. I hope I don't give in to a face lift. You know, a very old lady came up to me once. She looked up into my face, peered up to me, and she said in a sweet old voice, "I hate you." She had a very tightly stretched face, her eyes were like tiny slivers stretched up into her temples and there was barely any nose at all. Just two tiny pinpricks. I was not certain if the face might come unglued and fling itself at me. She said, "Well, do I look old?" I said, "No, madame, you look terrified." She was so aghast at my answer that she opened her mouth too wide and the face snapped and sprung loose! It zoomed around the room like a balloon when you let the air out of it. It smacked against the wall, and landed in a rubbery ball on the floor. Her driver ran over—we were at Armani's on Rodeo Drive—and he scooped it up into his palm. Then they rushed into a dressing room. She emerged somewhat intact, enough to make it out to her limo with some shred of dignity.

RF: I guess you don't need notes to remember something like that.

BSK: No. It stayed with me. I would like to have a very lined and wrinkled face when I am old, a noble face, a face that tells a story. The kind of face still fearful of death, but does not look upon it so garishly, you know.

RF: Some day you will give up your kittendom, then?

BSK: Is there a choice? I do the best I can. What else can anyone do? To have lived and loved, to have responded to the world with passion and not indifference, that is what I want. I want to have tasted all the ingredients at the salad bar, okay? When you get to the end, and you lift the ladle with your choice of dressing, that's it. What's on your plate tells your story.

As you know, I started to watch PBS to find out about cosmetic surgery. I never saw anything about it. And whenever they played something good, they asked for money. Because it's educational? I never dreamed of paying for an education. But I guess I learned something. And whenever I take in knowledge I do a breathing exercise. You can do it too.

Stand with your knees in the locked position. Breathe in your knowledge. Deep . . . deeper . . . breathe it in . . . hold that breath . . . hold it . . . aaannnd . . . blow it out! Nice and big. Let it go, release the knowledge, shake it out. Repeat, and proceed with your life.

—Pat Stevens

SEDWICKE-HARDWICK-WICKE PRESENTS THE AMERICAN TRAGEDY SERIES

Channel P England

Harpo, Illinois: An American Tragedy

"I'm a singer. I have a gift. When someone has a gift, they need to share it. They crave to share it. But that's a difficult thing to do in this town. Getting a break in this town is one in a million."

The voice of Rita Frittes, unemployed scat singer, Harpo, Illinois. Population, six. People. An American tragedy we meant to bring home with us to England, on film, for Channel P. Looking for the

Rita Frittes

death of small-town American life in the twentieth century, I arrived with my crew of twelve to talk with these people, isolated loners in a shrinking world. Harpo was crisp and quiet on this early autumn afternoon. I spoke with Rita through her kitchen window.

"You know, people think I'm lazy, or that I should give up here. But these are my roots. This is what I scat about. I can't leave. I've been looking for a gig in this town for fifteen years. There are no clubs. *No clubs!* Ask Freddy boy. He had the opportunity to open a club and he chose to open the Triple Scoop. Three guesses what that is. And I was married to him at the time. That killed me. Hard to fly after something like that happens."

Then, through a dusty puff of Viceroy smoke, a lilting voice emerged . . .

"Come fly with me, come fly with me, come fly fly fly fly fly . . ."

I headed toward the Triple Scoop, but was sidetracked by a young woman, a street tough in her early twenties. Her leopard stretch pants and brown toggle-button coat were a strange juxtaposition against this ghost town of moth-eaten structures and weeping willows. Her name was simply The Leopard.

"Hey, what do you want from me? You gonna shake me down, bust my jones, what? I'm clean, I tell ya. You got nothin' on me, pigs."

"Heavens no," I said, "I'm doing a documentary for Channel P, England. About the American Tragedy. Will you speak with us?"

"I'm a junkie, man. I'm *the* American tragedy, ya know. Don't let any other tragedy tell you different. I gotta cop, I gotta score, I got junk on my brain, junk on my mind, junk on my hair. Junk! Dig? Do you understand? That's what I live for. *Junk.* I gotta monkey on my back I gotta feed. It eats crack, it eats junk. I need weed, whack, what? What are you lookin' at?"

"I think I understand. You're a junkie."

"Yeah. But I ain't never scored, dig? That's the tragedy here. No drugs. I need to feed my kick and it ain't never eaten yet, dig? Look around you. This is a junkie's nightmare."

Yes, it was indeed a nightmare. No traffic, no people. No businesses, except the Triple Scoop, its large ice cream cone a weird juxtaposition against the leopard-skin pants with the brown toggle-button coat whose need for junk had become a desperation, an escape route out of the American Tragedy. "Let's go for some ice cream," I said. The crew followed. Behind us, the desperate cries of a small-town American junkie came at us like darts in a dart board game.

"I'm sick! I'm smacked! I'm dusted, dig?"

Knowing we could not help, we walked on. A woman in a black slip and fuzzy white sweater approached us. She beckoned us to follow her and we did. She led us to a cement slab posing as a front porch, in dire need of an Adirondack chair. She sat on a threadbare leather recliner in front of a weather-worn structure in need of a new door and windows. The American Tragedy spoke ever so clearly here.

"In 1964, Mae June Rooney stole some butter from our family. She came in through the kitchen door and stole it. My mother confronted her about it later, and she lied. She denied it like a rug. Mae June died about ten years later, and we found the butter in her refrigerator. She never admitted to it, but she was disgraced in death. We're the ones who have to live with it, though. We've lived with it for twenty years. It doesn't go away. By the way, my name is Mittens, but you can call me Kit. I've got an adjustable bed inside."

Mittens winked and then her eyes glazed over, as if she were reliving the nightmare. The American

Tragedy had taken hold. I directed the crew toward our destination, the Triple Scoop. Somehow I felt the answer to our quest lay there, perhaps with a busboy. We spotted a little boy in the street, about five years old with a head like a crystal ball.

"Hear that train comin'?" he asked us. "I do."

Inside, Fred Baldwin was behind his counter.

"People in this town are lazy. Take Rita. Singer? Ha. None of 'em can do a thing. Look at me. I'm successful. Why? Because I put my best foot forward, leave the other one lag behind. I don't ask too much of myself, and I won't settle for too little. That's the key. I do not choose to dream, I choose to remember what I have dreamt. That's my philosophy."

Fred Baldwin. Soda jerk. A man who found a part of himself and settled for it. Another American Tragedy. The little boy came in and parked his global shaped head at the counter. Knowingly, Fred set down a soda in front of him and watched the boy drink it.

"Population of Harpo is six, six people. We had eight people in this town until two people died on the same day. That just about sent the town into a tailspin. So I ran a special. Hot fudge sundaes. Sold twelve."

"Hear that train, Dad?" the boy asked. "I do."

Fred Baldwin

Small-town America was almost dead. A wide stretch of open field behind a neat white house with a tiny wooden front porch was covered with a carpet of curly yellow leaves. I did not hear a train, but I remembered our family dog. He would shake and whine hours before a thunderstorm. Warning us. Somehow this little boy, calm as a cucumber, knew something about our family dog.

We ascended the steps of the neat white house. Behind the screen door, a woman's voice deadpanned:

"Oh, yeah, I was married to Fred. Yahoo. What of it? Why should I talk about it to TV? What show are you, '911'? 'America's Funniest Home Videos'? Fred had one thing on his mind. Fred. Then he had two things on his mind, Fred and Rita. Scat! Get it?"

Another American nightmare. The voice continued.

"Boy, I can't wait for the day I run into her. Judgment day. One day Fred and I were playing Pictionary, the next day I'm playing solitaire. Don't you think it hurts me to know that I can't walk into that soda fountain and order a sundae like a man? Makes me weak. There's memories papered all over this town for me."

The screen door stopped speaking. We returned to Mittens's cement stoop.

"That Mae June . . . she stole some bacon from us once too. Fried bacon, coolin' on our window ledge. I'll never forget it either because we were gonna have BLTs. You know what that's like, going out to the kitchen to the smell of fried bacon, looking forward to bacon, lettuce, and tomato on white toast with mayonnaise? Maybe not, you're foreigners. All I found was a grease-soaked napkin . . . and that lingering smell. You can't replace something like that, not the same day."

Mittens's words lingered with the smell of bacon. I broke the crew for egg-salad sandwiches. We headed over to the Triple Scoop. The leopard-skin pants were still working the street.

"A junkie cannot be trusted. You lend us something, we will not return it. Junk comes first. You give me a sip of your pop, I'm gonna keep the bottle and return it for a deposit. You won't see the money or the bottle again. Understand? That's the way the junkie mind works."

We hurried inside. Fred spoke.

"Yeah, I have been involved with every woman here. All of 'em. I have a son. I can't be one hundred percent sure who the mother is. Not a woman in this town has stepped forward. With Rita, her career

Mittens

always came first. But the others, I clearly don't know why they haven't stepped forward. Mittens . . . that bed of hers nearly crippled me for life. And Lomita. Try to make love to a woman through a screen door! First it was Monopoly, and she was after me to get ahead. Then it was Scrabble and she wanted me to be smart. Then that damn picture game. I'm supposed to be some kind of artist. Lord. Spoke to The Leopard? Whew. She wanted me to be her pimp, even though I'm the only man in this town. She just didn't get it."

"What about your son? Will he stay in Harpo? What does the future hold for him here?"

"The honest truth? I don't know. I don't know if there will be anything for my son."

Outside, the voice of Rita Frittes drifted lazily into the street, then settled like dust. But it stirred up again when the boy threw a ball along the side of the road. It landed with a lonely thud and he chased after it, throwing it again, to no one. A harvest moon would soon hang like a Christmas tree ornament over the town of Harpo, delicately lighting up this American Tragedy. We had to head on. Rita's voice rose, and then I heard the train coming.

Our crew and I embarked on our next adventure— the urban nightmare. Another side of the American

Tragedy. As we directed our feelers toward the city, Harpo disappeared behind us, and the shadow of the structure that replaced its heartbeat fell across the gravel-studded road: the Shopping Mall. The rolling hills of corn and bean, some soy, some green, shrank behind us. Beige sharp-edged clusters of generic things began to populate our midst. The grasslands, once grass, were now occasionally patched with parking lots that surrounded the indoor shopping plaza or commercial office complexes. I broke the crew for breakfast at a mini-mart—bottles of juice, sugared rolls, coffee with a milky substance called "Non." We ate our fill of the American Dream, then headed onward, toward the tiny slabs of skyscrapers, which evoked images of tombstones in the distance. Ah yes, an American city awaited us.

We met our first interviewee outside a steak-and-egger, scanning what he would later refer to as his lost kingdom, a neighborhood rife with the changes of the monied young.

"These people say they're buying the neighborhood, but they're not. They're stealing it, fair and square."

He's known simply as Joe, the Janitor. Here he stands, the American Gothic, except that his pitchfork is a push broom, there is no plain, staunch woman beside him, and the background is not a farmhouse, it's a coffee shop called the Buzzing Fly. It is here that Joe has his cup of jo, his java, light or dark, Boston, with or without, here or to go. It is here he eats his cherry or cheese danish, his sunny side up with hashbrowns, American fries, dark toast, burn the bacon, Adam and Eve on a raft naked, shoot a pair, hold the mayo, short stack, whiskey down. This was his language, the ancient jive of a lower-middle-class barrio. This was working-class talk, spoken in a thin midwestern twang.

"I grew up here. Dreamland, right? My dream was to die right here, but maybe I was asking too much. These—let's be kind and call 'em jerks. These jerks, they're destroying everything, the face of the whole neighborhood, just because it's got a few wrinkles."

We asked Joe if gentrification isn't a renewal. Isn't it a healing, a way of restoring new life to an old neighborhood?

"The only people who can breathe here are *them*. The rest of us can't afford the air. They're driving people out like cattle with money they stole from the farmers. And they won't be happy until we're all sandblasted along with the brick. The only thing they didn't fix is the grade school. They haven't done a thing to improve that. They come into the Fly and order strange things, want to know if the beef we serve ate chemicals. I'd like to ask them what the hell they think their brand new car is dishing up for Chrissake. And they tell me these people are educated. We ask these people to kindly leave the coffee shop, as in *Beat it!* I love to see 'em slink outta here with their tails between their legs. Makes my day."

Is Joe resentful?

"I believe the Pope's Catholic, isn't he? I'm sick. These people make me sick, they make me feel like I've got the flu. They've got their credit cards, but they're no good in the Fly. In the old days we paid cash, and if we didn't have the cash we wrote a bad check. They had no way to check up on you then, so they had to trust you. Now that's a thing of the past. We used to tuck our savings under a mattress or in a shoe box because we didn't want anybody to know we had anything. These people, they tell the world. It's *me me me!* They even wear T-shirts that say ME on the front. Good. Now the snipers will know who to shoot at. I wear dull colors, you know, your browns and your grays, so I'm not an easy target in the city. But these people—bull's-eye! I wish I was going to be here in thirty, forty years when their rents are twenty thousand a month and they can't come up with it. Oh, boy. They'll be renting space in somebody's Weber grill. And their kids won't be home for dinner on Sundays, know why? 'Cause they'll be living on Mars. Get it, Mom and Dad? *We—hate—you!*"

We asked Joe how long he'd lived in the neighborhood.

"Since I was four. Fifty-seven years. It's called Little Ukrania, but we got Russian, German, some Italian, a few Irish I think. No Hispanic. They live in Hispanic World or Little Hispania, something like that. It's about three miles north of here. These buildings you see around here, they were built by bricklayers. With their hands. Solid. The streets are brick too, underneath the tar."

"So you're saying different kinds of people have settled in the neighborhood over the years."

"Yeah, but they didn't change it. They didn't mind the flaws. They became the flaws, you know? They were grateful. These new people, they treat the neighborhood like it ain't got no memories, like it has no sacred grounds. They think the bingo hall's a joke. They peer into it like that and snicker. Like it's a joke. You wanna hear a joke? My mother won five hundred dollars in that bingo hall in 1978. Laugh, why don't ya. Five hundred dollars. She bought patio furniture for the first time in her life. And she died on that patio furniture, layin' in the backyard one night that summer, under a bed of stars. They says it was either a massive stroke or from a lot of mosquito bites, they don't know which happened first. But I know what she died of. Contentment. God save her soul. On a chaise longue. Her dream come true."

"What will Joe die of?" I asked. But before Joe could answer, the piercing cry of a BMW shattered the urban stillness. It was a car alarm, the ultimate symbol of the capitalist mythology. In a different time, in a different community, an alarm would bring out the townspeople. It was a warning—fire, tornado, the British. But this was not that warning. It was a shrill reminder that chanted its gentrified mantra over and over and over. To Joe and the other older inhabitants of the barrio, it signaled an end of an era. Joe shook his head and walked on, his American dream squished in the backs of his work shoes.

Lucky and Mahoney Real Estate, 9:42 A.M.

"You talked to Joe? Colorful character, isn't he? That's part of the reason people are falling in love with the area. And we're preserving that quality. Lots of people don't understand that because the prices are high. Welcome to reality. The demand is astonishing. And these buildings are old. We don't build 'em like this no more. Sure we fix 'em up. Add a deck, a skylight, that sort of thing. You turn sixty something you get a face lift, right? We're treating the buildings like we treat ourselves. Nobody likes to get old, we realize that. We like to see the older ones around. Ambience. Yes, it sounds cold. I got parents too, you know. But I'm a real estate developer. Affluence always breeds some kind of contempt. The businesses here have been replaced with something different; they have to cater to who's coming in here now. That makes sense.

We asked Lucky about the new buildings going up, those that are out of *character*, as he put it, with Joe's brick-layed buildings.

"The land value is outtasight. There's been empty lots around here for years. They never did anything with them. There were fifty varieties of weeds in one lot we just sold. Fifty. Now that's neglect. We're working on a deal to buy the Catholic Church—Saint Ambrose, huge place, beautiful. We're going to get Helmut Schmitboff to redesign it. German architect. Dynamite loft apartments, ultra modern, ultra luxury. Wait till the press gets aholda that. The civic groups will be after our asses. It'll be a hell of a fight. These people don't see the danger in organized religion."

Lucky laughed and his suit shone brightly, maybe like the stars that filled the sky over Joe's mother the night she realized her American Dream.

"Would you guys like an iced cappuccino? Cranberry spritzer? Anything? A Coke? That's what I need. Jill!"

We asked Lucky about the beauty shop up the street with its Day-Glo orange FOR SALE sign screwed into its brick wall.

"Oh, yeah. Fasta Pasta's comin' in there. The whacko who's in there now's been there since eternity, if you believe in eternity. She's nuts. But you'll love her. A real character."

We walked two doors up the street and entered a door below the hanging sign, THE BRUSH STROKE. The shop was empty of people but filled with a menagerie of articles, figurines, knickknacks, bric-a-brac. Trinkets on the bracelet of a middle-class dream.

"Hello? Anybody home? Channel P England, we have an appointment." A woman stepped through layers of drapery, as if out of some surreal storybook.

"Sorry, I was in the ladies room."

It was Estelle. Tight black headdress, dark glasses, thin black dress, and red-striped jacket. She was a character indeed. We asked about Lucky and his quest to get her out of the shop.

"Yes, he wants to turn it into a pasta house or something. That's nice. But you know I've been here twenty-two years and some of my customers haven't died yet. Lucky questions my work, and that bothers me. Nobody's ever done that. My ladies don't come here just for a hairdo. It's a club. We eat chocolates, talk, drink coffee. Lately it's been decaf—we're not totally immune to change as people think we are. I do funeral services here too. That's what he objects to. Says I've got two businesses going, but I don't. It's all the same thing."

"How did you go from beauty shop to mortuary?"

"I'm not a mortician. I'm an artist. I went to the Art Institute years ago, before it was a good school. The hairdos I create are sculpture; you should see them. I don't *do* banana curls, I comment on them. Women walk out of here with strong statements on their heads, visions of sugar plums dancing and so forth. It's a fantasy surrounding your face, your brain, your universe, if you will. A French twist becomes a bear claw, a plain bun becomes an eclair, a ponytail becomes a cascading fountain of youth."

"But you mentioned funerals."

"One day I had three ladies in the shop. It suddenly dawned on me that Kay had been under the drier for three hours. Every time I looked over at her, she was flipping through the pages of her magazine, so I went on sculpting. Then I noticed that

106

she wasn't really flipping the pages, it was the fan blowing them, making her of course look very much alive. I said to Marie, 'Excuse me,' and went over to Kay, lifted the drier, and discovered she was deceased. Her hair was brittle, like peanut brittle—a perm cannot take that kind of heat—and well, I felt terrible, responsible on so many levels. So, we agreed; I had the services right here in the shop. After that, everybody wanted it that way."

"How many services have you had in the shop?"

"Oh, many, many, though I don't keep track. People come to me, they bring their pets. You cannot believe it, what people want. Vic and Carol, dear friends, came to me, grieving. Their little dog, Peanut, a Chihuahua, died of obesity. Well, I was never very fond of the dog, always parading past the shop in a new outfit, usually skintight. If he only knew how silly he looked . . . but Vic and Carol were dear friends, so I said I would do something. Well, they're of the Catholic persuasion, so I went to a religious-goods store, and I found an Infant of Prague outfit. This is a statue that has a collection of clothes, like Barbie. Beautiful things, and very expensive. I found a red velvet cloak, a white satin tunic type of thing with an empire waist, a scepter, and a crown, and I brought it back to the shop and did a fitting. Well, I was all day taking out darts.

Peanut was quite overweight, you see. But finally I got him in it and, well, he looked like a bishop or a cardinal or something. Very impressive. I don't know what kind of maker a dog meets when he passes on, but Peanut was definitely getting through the gates somewhere. When Vic and Carol saw him, they burst forth in their grief and joy. This was a dog that bit people's ankles—really a terrible little creature—but he looked like a prince. I did it because I cared for my friends. A lot of people in the neighborhood didn't understand that."

"Do your regular costumers resent the fact that you do services for animals too?"

"No. They bring their pets to me too. You should have seen Joyce's parakeet, Tony Bennett. I put a little toupee on its head, dressed him in a dark suit, and stood him next to a miniature piano. We played Tony's 'Rags to Riches,' and from a distance he looked exactly like Tony Bennett. He *was* Tony. Of course, the bird never sounded that good. We cried. People love their pets with a different kind of abandon than they love human beings. The relationships aren't complex, but the grief is real, it's innocent."

"What will happen if you have to leave the shop? There's so much history here, obviously."

"Whether I stay or go my work will go on. We talk, we drink our coffee, we eat our Fanny May. We love each other, I guess. We have an understanding. There is beauty and there is death, and even in death there is beauty. And it's the same for everybody. It's simple."

We left Estelle in her otherworldly domain-for-sale. Two ladies approached the shop as we did so, chattering like magpies in the morning. With our cameras we peered into the neighborhood's yards, gardens dotted with statuettes and birdhouses. Here a Blessed Mother in a bathtub, there a Francis of Assisi, robins and sparrows splashing in the birdbath he balanced on his head. We came upon a very old man in his garden, leaning over an antique pushcart filled with poppies and azaleas and geraniums and sweet pea. We called to him.

"Channel P, England, sir. Will you speak with us about the American Tragedy?"

But he shook his head, and in a broken accent said, "I don't speak English." An old woman was approaching him with a glass of lemonade. We didn't bother to ask her for an interview, lest we uncover another American Disappointment. Better to leave them in their world of whirligigs and isolation.

We walked through the neighborhood toward our van. Evening was approaching. Muumuus faded and flowered smocks dimmed with the changing light. Occasionally, the neighborhood characters could be seen on their front porches, drinking cans of beer or glasses of iced tea. Somewhere someone was playing an accordion, which merged with yet other sounds in the not so distant distance: the buzz saw, the hammer. The future was coming. Somebody was building a new addition onto the American Dream.

Enchanted with the disenchantment we had found, my crew and I returned to Mother England, and Channel P. We would not forget Harpo and Little Ukrania. We would sort through our film footage on the ravages of progress, time, and change. We would edit the Great American Wilderness. Before we left the United States we talked to Joe once more. He was sweeping out a hallway, muttering something under his breath. We reminded him that his beloved brick streets were once dirt roads tread on by horses' hoofs. That that same road was an Indian trail, sacred burial grounds, a prairie, a place where the buffalo roamed, and where dinosaurs stalked.

For a moment Joe looked perplexed, reflective. Then he said, "If the dinosaurs got a million years, and the Indians got a hundred thousand, how come I only get fifty-seven?"

Indeed.

2 | Life Without Legs

THE BALLAD OF
A BROASTED WOMAN

*T*here was a time when great creative waves rolled off the Atlantic, right between my toes, and I carved egrets out of moist driftwood pieces and made abstract owls from the many bits of broken shell the sea brings in. Life was in abundance.

That was then.

I live still in a tiny seashore town in southern New Jersey. One would not think a tiny seashore town existed in southern New Jersey, but it does. And I do. Sort of. I am just a shell of my former self.

I'm a drinker. If I were a man they'd call me a drunk or a bum. But I'm a woman so I'm a lush. I'm surprised you can read this. It's written in a slur. I've crawled out of a few whiskey bottles in my time, only to plunge myself back into a frozen daiquiri. Nobody calls a frothy blended drinker a drunk do they? But when they find you shimmying up the straw of their Brandy Alexander, they want answers.

"Lois, what are you doing here?"

"Buy me one, Taffy," I say, "Casey's cut me off."

"Now Lois," says Taffy, a big woman, "I could drink you under the table, but why should I? It's a waste of life time. Casey's cut you off for a good reason."

"Aw, come on, Taffy," I plead. But she shakes her head.

"How 'bout you, Harvey?" Harvey's got a radio show, my favorite. I listen every evening. "Come on, Harvey, play me my favorite drink, will ya? Please. Don't make me beg, 'cause you know I will."

But Harvey says no go and I slide back down the straw into frothy oblivion.

I wasn't always this way. I didn't always live here, either. And what a lot of people forget about a hard drinkin' woman like me, a dyed dark-blue brunette of fifty or so, when they see me in a board-walk bar in Sea Isle City or strutting my stuff at the Liquor Tree in Wildwood, what they forget is I've got a past, and a family.

My mother is the late sculptress Edna Gandy from Dubois, Pennsylvania. She had her heyday in the sixties, rising to prominence with her bronze bust entitled *Generation.* During every exhibition she would carry the bust from room to room, setting it down and picking it up again, explaining, "People don't know where their heads are at."

My father was born in Twist, Washington. He was the man who raised buffoonery to its cult status in the sixties. He ran for President every off election year, and he served two days in jail for wearing a polyester American flag dashiki. His name was Garfield Stoote, and he was a famous pacifist who later wrote murder mysteries. His first was a bestseller, his second killed him.

That leaves my brother, Edgar, named so for Edna and Garfield. He was born without legs, but don't pity him. He got every bit of sympathy and renown for it that he deserved, and more. He got all the attention my parents' well-fed egos could mete out. There was nothing left for me, born two years later. Lois. Who am I named for? Nobody. The *L* stands for Lost and Loose. Or Legs—the one with.

And as I grew older, my curse expanded; for not only did I have legs, I had great legs.

I was born independent. I walked at three

months. "Look, Mom and Dad! Look what I can do with these!" But they did not notice me. I painted wildly colorful abstract renditions of my anxiousness and taped them to the refrigerator. My parents told me to clean up the mess and gave me a pair of white cowgirl boots and a baton. You've got legs, they said. March!

"But I'm an abstract artist!" I cried.

Clearly I did not interest them. For my mother it was the shape of her career and her latest sculpture that interested her. For my father it was himself. For both of them, it was Edgar, their utterly unique bizarre invention. Edgar *was* abstract art.

"Taffy, please, won'tcha buy me just one little itsy-bitsy teeny-weeny Tanqueray martini? Pretty pretty pretty please . . . I'm beggin' ya."

I didn't always beg, and I didn't always live here in this seashore town. I was once the mistress of a grand apartment on Lake Shore Drive with a picture window framing the Great Lake Michigan. My husband Jimmy was heir to a dry-cleaning fortune and I was a social martini. Every night when Jimmy got home from the office, I'd mix us each a perfect combination of gin and vermouth in a crystal pitcher, pour it into two crystal martini glasses, and plunk a big fat anchovy olive in each. Then one evening, ten years before his time, Jimmy came home, hung up his hat, and keeled over. I mixed myself a Tanqueray martini, checked his pulse, and called the paramedics.

After everything was sorted out, I was a rich woman. I decided to fulfill my dream to be a free-spirited abstract artist, living in a beach house on the beach, you know, like Liz Taylor in *The Sandpiper.* I packed a bulky knit sweater and a two-piece bathing suit, and headed off for the Great Salty.

My beach house was lovely, and still is, even though I see it through different eyes now. Unlike the spotted owl of Oregon, the shattered-shell owl of southern New Jersey thrives here, in my cabin on the ocean. They line the steep set of stairs that lead to the deck. They sit on every table and on the toilet tank lid and hang over every doorway and on every poster of my four-poster bed. Friends often told me to get rid of them—they gave a person the heebie-jeebies. My work was considered representational, not abstract at all.

But I had found my identity. I had sprouted wings. My owls and my driftwood egrets were the rebirth of my free spirit.

My life as an artist was built like a sandcastle, vulnerable to the tide and to insensitive people who stepped on it deliberately or not. As I was fashioning my life as a real artist, Edgar was building a name for himself as a crass commercialist in Cape May. A sketch artist. A painter of realistic waves and sea gulls. Oh my, how the tourists marveled. Look at what the man without legs can do! Now, I'm willing to marvel at an artist who has no arms and who paints with his toes, but my Lord, what choice did Edgar have? And how he soaked up the attention. Like a Coppertone tan. My father would come to Edgar's shows in Egg Harbor without even a phone call to me and my egrets. Edgar became the Toast of Tuckahoe, and my father was there, in a dinner jacket, grabbing what glory he could.

So, the sands sifted. I lived out my adulthood as I had my childhood. Lois the Lonely. Oh, I had friends and lovers, but as the years went on, I preferred to be alone, to watch the sun disappear over the marshlands while I sipped martinis and ate batches of homemade broasted chicken. You can't find broasted chicken on the east coast, you know. In fact, Chicago is the only place that I've ever known to have it. I guess it's an indecisive midwestern delicacy, a combination of roasted and broiled chicken. The only time my father ever took me out for dinner, we had broasted chicken, and it is for that reason that I now prepare it on special occasions. Like Wednesdays.

While Edgar's popularity grew, I became more reclusive. Occasionally, when the sea beckoned, I would answer it, and when in the mood I would perform a striptease for a flock of gulls. They were wildly appreciative. But I didn't go out. Why? Because everywhere I went I was Edgar's sister. Garfield's daughter. The recluse weirdo who collects clam shells. The big flop without any talent. It was Edgar this and Edgar that. Edgar and Garfield at every party. An Edgar Stoote on every wall. His paintings sold as fast as flapjacks at a firehouse breakfast, but for me all of the paintings were missing something. You know, blueberries.

And there was talk, about my lovers and my drinking. They said if it wasn't for my great legs and my money, I never would have been awarded so many admirers. But I measured my own success. It made me suspicious and unpopular. So I was happy when I was alone.

Finally Edgar's popularity waned. His new batch of pancakes weren't selling. Garfield moved back to Minnesota. Edgar was desperate for the attention to which he was accustomed and, in my opinion, desperate to convince himself he was indeed an important artist. So one afternoon he went out to the dunes and lobbed off an ear. Then, in utter artistic agony, a pinky. The locals took interest and his sales shot back up again. He was riding the wave once more, the darling of the Beesley's Point art set.

Not much later came the news of our father's death. Estranged for twenty years, I had only spoken to my father after he and Edgar's latest and last publicity stunt together, which I had completely ignored.

I told you my father wrote murder mysteries. The first was well received, and had garnered him a new cult following. Of course. The second was his masterpiece, a six-hundred-page potboiler. He considered it the whodunit of the century. I read it as soon as it hit the newsstands, and indeed, it was a cliff-hanging thriller of considerable merit. I read it for three days and three nights, on the edge of my seat, to find out who done it. The end was a shocker. The culprit was my father, Garfield Stoote!

My father claimed that the whole book was true, and insisted he be arrested, which he was—for murder. Though there was no evidence, and no body, the FBI was only too glad to get their hands back on the ex-radical clown of the sixties. His trial was a circus, with Edgar in attendance every day. With no legs, one ear, and minus a finger, he was everything Garfield Stoote's son should be, and the media feasted. Edgar had a show in Minneapolis, and became the art darling of the Twin Cities.

Lois the Lonely sat on her deck, eating her broasted chicken, and reading the news stories, which were buried each morning in the pages of the *New York Times.*

The jury found the book and the charges to be fictional, and my father was cleared. At his post-trial press conference he said that all of our lives were fictional, and are made relevant only through our own inventions. Those of us with rich, active imaginations are closer to the truth, the truth being the stories we share and tell. That is what links us together, the organic antidote for human isolation. Then he signed a three-million-dollar book-and-movie deal, and hit the road.

I stayed home and examined my own inventions. The eyes of my egrets and owls watched me, but they would not tell me the truth.

Edgar returned to Tuckahoe a hero, and to a huge reception, which I attended. When the big flop sister got drunk and planted a sloppy kiss on her brother's mouth, he ordered her in disgust to leave. She disrobed, and did so. That is one of the many benefits of alcohol.

My father called me the next day and asked me to take a trip with him to the West Indies. He planned to write his book on an island. Apparently this latest episode had made him look at his life and desire to rearrange it. I said no. He called me every day for a week, begging me to be his daughter again, and for a chance to make things up to me.

"I heard you have nice legs," he told me. "I'd love to see them."

But bitterness had taken hold. Sometimes it's just too late, the sun's coming up, the party's over. So I stuck to my answer, and my father was killed. By a fanatical murder-mystery cultess who found a passage of his book offensive to her and her brother.

Instead of a trip to the Caribbean there was a grand funeral, attended by every nut-whacko-artist-nitwit from my parents' era. And Edgar. He became my father's spirit's alter ego. I did not attend.

That's the day I started to frequent the Liquor Tree. That's the day I dove into the daiquiri.

You know, I love the summers down here. Unlike the other so-called locals, those people who identify only within the proximity of the General Store, I like it when the vacationers arrive. I like to watch the babies waddle on the beach. I like to sit in Feeney's Merry-Go-Round Pub in the afternoons, drinking cans of beer, mingling with the other drinkers in our unfocused world. Then I come home to my deck, and at five o'clock I mix myself a Tanqueray martini. My organic link to Jimmy. "Here's to me," I say, and I toast myself and my cockeyed ocean. It's always been cold in Edgar's shadow, even if it only covers half of me. That's why I like my deck. The wood is warm. I turn the radio on in the kitchen so I can hear Harvey's show, "High Tide with Harvey." He plays Doris Day. I suck on a big fat gin-soaked anchovy olive and prop my sandy feet up on the patio table. Why not? Who's to complain? I'm alone here, and I've got a great set of gams.

AMBROSIA: LIZ SWEENEY TALKS WITH HARVEY LATSIS

*H*ey everybody. Hello hello. I'm Harvey Latsis. Welcome to 'High Tide with Harvey,' serving the shore, from the Tuckahoe Inn to the sunken ship in Cape May. And folks, if you're visiting the area, welcome, and make sure you get on down and see that attraction at the Cape, right down there at the lighthouse. But boy oh boy, for the rest of us a little hammock swayin's in order, huh? So ask the wife to brew you up a nice fresh glass of iced tea, and suspend yourself over that lawn you ought to be mowin'. Ha ha. . . . We've got Doris Day, so hang on in there, Lois, I know you're lis-

Liz Sweeney

tening. We've got Peggy Lee, and we've got a real special treat, live in our studio, Liz Sweeney. That's right, one half of that famous duo. She's back in Beesley's Point. And she's gonna chat away with us while the little lady fixes that tea or whatever the heck is goin' on out there. Or is it goin' down. What are they saying these days? I can never keep up. Boy oh boy, Liz, hard to keep up with you too. You've gone solo now, have you? And you are over at the Ground Chuck on Hawksnest Road."

"Well, Harvey, I have gone solo, but I'm not singing. I'm a hostess! And I love it. It's nice to be back in the area, especially without all the pressures attached to performing. I was driving up Shore Road and I couldn't help but slow down at the A.M./P.M. Motel."

"Oh, yeah, the old A and P we called it. . . . We sure did have some times there . . . holy mackerel. But there wasn't a lounge there, was there?"

"No. Just the motel. We used to do our sets in front of the check-in counter. The audience would spill right out into the parking lot."

"Well, I guess they'd have to. . . . And as I recall, you played early check-in as well."

"Boy, you've got a memory!"

"It's right under my toupee! Ha ha ha ha ha ha . . . ha ha ha ha ha. You also played the Crab Trap. During the off season."

"We sure did. You get a different crowd when the crabs are out of season. Intimate. Small. Very small. We've always been partial to that kind of crowd. And I think our medleys kept it that way through the years."

"Boy they sure did. Liz, let's go down memory lane, and boy it's a long one."

"Watch out. Don't get me crying—my mascara will run and I'll never catch it. I'm getting too old!"

"Ha ha ha ha ha ha . . . ha ha ha ha ha ha ha . . . ha ha ha ha ha. Oh, boy. Let me catch my breath. I'm getting too old for that too! Where were we? I've lost my place."

"As I recall, I used to put you in your place every Saturday night!"

"Oh, boy, I've got some explaining to do now, folks. Liz and I are old friends, but we were just friends. Coupla times I may have gotten a little fresh, and Liz reminded me I was married."

"Three times!"

"Correct! All wonderful gals by the way. Hello if you're listening. So . . . the interview. I'm having too much fun. What was your most memorable gig? Is that what you call it these days?"

"It is. Exactly. That's a toughy. Let's see . . . I'd have to say it was our last stand, so to speak. Our last engagement was in Wilke, Nebraska, where we did six weeks at the Think and Drink, right there next to Gomez Field. We were touring airport lounges. [Applause.] Thank you! You're very kind."

"Listeners, that was a bit of acknowledgment from Ed Smors, our engineer here. He's been to quite a few airport lounges. Thanks, Ed. Fly boy, huh? Heh heh. . . . Boy, how do ya play with those engines roaring overhead?"

"Well first of all, it was a small airport. Only two flights a day go out of Gomez, and one's a mail run up to Lowport, so if nobody's sending a postcard, the plane stays right there until somebody does! We played the late afternoon slot, two to two-thirty."

"Wow. That's a tough draw."

"Not for us, Harvey. We papered the house every day. Every stool was occupied. These are beautiful, loyal fans out there in Wilke. Granted, we had some overflow from the snack bar, but we had eighteen to twenty people at every set. All people from the Wilke area, mostly unemployed, people without work. Part of the reality of Gomez, and the attraction, I guess. There were a few fellas with a drinking problem, and a gal or two. I don't deny that. But you know, during our medley, they didn't need a drink."

"So in a way, you became their cocktail."

"Yes. I was a Sloe Gin Fizz!"

"Ha ha ha ha ha ha ha . . . hah ha ha ha ha ha. But I never thought of you as slow."

"Thank you. I'll take that as a compliment. And I remember a particular evening at Wee Willie Winkies when you were a Harvey Wallbanger!"

"Yes indeed, my namesake. Heh heh heh heh heh heh . . .

"Ha ha ha. We're having too much fun now. Arrest us! Take us away. Anyhow . . . I love the people out there in Wilke. Special hello to all the airport employees, that's Barb and Tom. Hello out there."

"I don't think our transmission goes out that far. Too bad. If anybody here in town knows Barb or Tom in Wilke, Nebraska, or if anybody is making a trip out to Wilke, pass on our greetings and salutations, will ya? Boy, nostalgia brings back memories, doesn't it?"

"So it does."

"Liz, let's get personal. You never married . . ."

"Not that I can remember, no. I was married to my career, Harvey. That takes its toll. Most of the men I was involved with were lounge singers as well, and you know, that was so emotionally taxing, there wasn't much left over for love in my life. We were on the road a lot, and our work was so sensual in its nature that we sometimes didn't have much of that left either. A good tune turns me on; taking bits and pieces and shaping them into the form of a medley turns me on. A good medley is like ambrosia."

"Now wait a minute. Ambrosia . . . isn't that when you can't remember something? Heh heh . . ."

"No, no . . . ambrosia's got marshmallows in it, I think. Or is it coconut. I can't remember."

"Maybe you've got ambrosia. Ha ha ha ha ha ha . . ."

"I guess it's a poor analogy. Fruit salad is more like it. Peel the banana and slice it, pluck the grapes, core and slice the apple. You've got to do that work or you won't get the salad. You won't get the medley. It's exciting. So I guess I didn't look hard enough for love, and the love I found didn't last."

"Okay. Let's talk about Larry LaFontaine."

[Long pause]. "That was one fruit medley that mixed for a long time. Larry . . . Larry LaFontaine . . ."

"Brother of Chick, one half of the LaFontaine Brothers."

"Yes. Larry and I fell for each other fast. I was attending a twentieth wedding anniversary, and he and Chick were the duo performing at the dance. When I walked in, he forgot the words to 'Born Free.' "

"Practically impossible, of course. My, you must have been a distraction."

"Sue me! I was. And so was he. That gorgeous head of hair. Well, I eventually got up on stage and joined them in, of all things, a medley. We sang 'Fame,' 'You Light Up My Life,' 'I Never Promised You a Rose Garden,' and 'Mandy.' "

"Manilow, right? I don't play much Manilow on the show. I just don't understand it."

"Pop with classical overtones. It's a complex mix. Anyhow, I actually went on the road with Chick and Larry, a bus tour. Two months. It was up and down, and I was causing quite a rift between the brothers, you know. I think Chick was jealous, and I don't blame him. Larry and I were always sneaking off for a donut and coffee, quote unquote. Chick wasn't born yesterday . . ."

"So Chick sort of put the kibosh on the whole thing."

"Well, yes, I guess so. We were doing a show on a bus to Grand Rapids, and suddenly, right in the middle of a number, Chick pulled Larry's hair off! We were doing 'Cracklin' Rosie.' I'll never forget Larry; he was really into the tune, you know. Reaching the crescendo and whoosh! This beautiful head of hair is yanked off his head and flung the length of the bus."

"Oh, my, and he had a head of hair, as you stated earlier."

"A woman who was sleeping at the time woke up and screamed—she thought it was a possum. You know sometimes out on those country roads you don't know what might get on the bus. Well, you know how everybody felt about Larry LaFontaine's hair—he built a career on it."

"Now when I mentioned my toupee earlier, folks, I was kidding. I had no idea you were going to spring this story on us, Liz. It's fascinating."

"Well, Larry's a better man for it. He's in a support group, and you know that isn't like him. He's grown because of the whole thing. I think he knows he can be accepted for who he is."

"He's bald. My gosh, what a tragedy."

"Well, it changed things between us. The lack of trust on his part. He never told me; he said he forgot."

"A little ambrosia on his part. Heh heh . . ."

"He and Chick are still together, though. They worked it out. There weren't that many people on the bus at the time."

"Let me say to the men out there listening: If you wear a hair piece and the little lady doesn't know about it, make sure it's glued on tight. Or come clean. Not worth breaking up a good thing over, if you know what I mean. So, have you found happiness now that you're not performing anymore?"

"I have, Harvey. I'm a people person, you know that. I need a lot of warm bodies around me, that's all I ask. I came back here to the shore because I always loved it. When you're on the road, you've got to carry your home with you everywhere you go, in your heart. So, I'm putting my heart where my home is."

"And you're working at the Ground Chuck. Boy, they do a lot of volume out there, don't they? Big place."

"You better believe it. Come on down sometime. We've got a Salisbury steak that'll knock your socks off, and every Salisbury steak dinner comes with a glass of champagne. Pink! My favorite. So come. Imbibe!"

"Sounds like a New Year's Eve idea. Any singing at all?"

"I never say never. I sometimes say no, a gal's got to, but I never say never."

"Thanks for stoppin' by, Liz, and we'll all see you at the Ground Chuck, out on Hawksnest Road. Big parking lot I understand, so go on down there and let Liz seat you."

"We've got a great seating system."

"All the tables are numbered on a chart, aren't they?"

"So there's no confusion, yes."

"Liz Sweeney. Okay . . . I'm gonna play a little Doris Day, she's gonna 'Face the Music and Dance.' That's for you, Lois. But before that, let me give you our Contest Question, the whole ball of marbles being a paid vacation to Hollywood, California, so listen up. What 1948 movie originated as a radio drama, and starred Barbara Stanwyck and Burt Lancaster? Our third caller will be our prize winner . . ."

LEW AND ALICE IN WONDERLAND

I never wanted to go nowhere really. If I want a vacation, I go to the park. I sit on a park bench next to a fountain and drink in the trees. I like my neighborhood. I like to stay in my own backyard. The grass is always greener over the fence, isn't it? But when you climb over there, you'll look in the next yard, and that will look greener too. And when you look in the next yard, you'll say, "Oh, I'd like to go over there." And once you're there, you'll see through the bushes and say, "Well, I'll just spend the day." And you'll go from yard to yard to yard to yard. Greener greener greener. Pretty soon you'll be five miles away from home and you won't have bus fare.

No, I like to stay close to home. That's where Alice is, my sister. We grew up together. I was a boy and she was a girl and that's all we had in common. Now I'm a man, fifty-five years old. But Alice is still like a baby. A bag baby. She lives outside.

I can honestly say that most of my life has been happy. Only last year a few things went wrong. I lost my wallet, my camera, and my sister. All in one day. The only thing I found was my sister, wouldn't you know it? At the supermarket, as usual. She likes to go to the supermarket, load up her basket with food, wheel it around the store like a big shot, and then put everything back. She never has no money, you see. The first thing she asked me was if I had my wallet.

I said, "Alice, I don't have any money for you. I lost my wallet."

Alice says very loud, "You'd lose your head if it wasn't examined!"

See what I mean?

When I lost my camera I was very upset. I said to myself, Listen, Lew . . . and if you can't be on a first-name basis with yourself, you may as well hang up your hat . . . listen, Lew, what can you do? Cry about it?

Crying won't help you. You don't have a camera no more. Now you just have to remember what you see. You don't have a wallet no more. Put something else in your pocket.

I do miss my camera. I miss my wallet too. Lucky for me I took a picture of it.

If there's one thing that's true, there's bound to be other things. Believe me. But for sure, one of those things is, Don't Look Back. Why should you? It's all spilled milk. When you spill milk, what do you do? You wipe up the mess and you hang up the towel. I don't look back. I know what's behind me. My wallet, my camera, and my sister. Of all of those things she's the only one who don't get lost. Even if she's two blocks behind me, she's always there.

I never wanted to go anywhere with Alice. It's not the way she looks or anything which puts some people off, even people at the restaurant where I work. She's not allowed to eat there, so she comes around back where I wash the dishes and I fix her a plate. Hand it to her through the back door the same way I would a squirrel or better yet a robin.

The only difference is she don't fly away. I wish she would.

I never asked to go nowhere with nobody. Alice or otherwise. Not even on a vacation. That's why what happened to me was such a shock.

I don't have a clock, you see. I used to have a clock but it stopped one day just like that. Don't look back, right? Spilled milk. I'm always ready to hang up the towel. When I really need the time, I just call on the telephone. Usually in the morning so I won't be late for work at the restaurant. One day I called up for the time and a man said, "Hello, this is 'High Tide with Harvey'! Do you have the Radio Waves contest answer?" I said, "Sorry, wrong number." Next thing you know, I'm goin' to Hollywood! And I have to bring somebody with me. Guess who?

That night I had a dream. It smelled like fruit punch.

We landed in California in the evening, me and Alice. She was all stiff because she had stayed in the overhead compartment most of the way, and then had stowed herself under the seat in front of her. Now she could barely walk. As usual, all kinds of scrap papers were pinned to her dress; our old address from when we were little, a note my mother wrote the grocer so Alice could buy cigarettes for her, a worn envelope that said *Alice's Lunch Money* on it, and her school photo from the fourth grade. She looked like a bulletin board.

Well, we went in a limousine to the best hotel in town, the Best Western, and we had a beautiful room, overlooking a pool the size of your fist. Magnificent! If only we had thought to bring our bathing suits. . . .

The first place Alice wanted to go was the supermarket. I said, "Alice how many supermarkets do you have to see in your lifetime before you know they're all the same." She didn't hear me. I said, "Okay, but first let's go in the car they gave us. Would you like that, Alice?"

Alice said real loud, "Don't talk to me like I'm a baby!"

But she sat with me in the car, watching the moonlight ripple across the waves in the pool. It was a nice moment really. We just sat there. We don't drive, we don't have our license. Then I said, "Alice, let's go see the movie stars and their houses tomorrow, first thing." I could see the hills off in the distance.

The next day we started up the street on foot toward the purple hills. You see, when I want something, I get it. Nothing can stop me. Like when I went to get the job at the pharmacy, they said they don't need anybody. "Oh, you don't?" I said. "Listen mister, and listen hard!" Then I walked out, steaming mad, just for effect you know. Two weeks later I come back, I said, "I'm gonna give you a second chance, understand? I'll work for free, but don't push me." I got that job in a second flat. And I still work there regular on a volunteer basis.

So we were headed for the hills. Boy oh boy, it was hot. I shouldn't have worn my parka. Alice was wearing four dresses, but that's not out of place for her. She's been known to wear all of her dresses at the same time. Calls herself a layer cake. It doesn't bother her but it drives other people crazy. It made our cousin Ginny real mad. Ginny said, "Alice, I'm going to stop giving you clothes if you wear all of them on the same day." Ginny's the one who's got a lot of money. If you asked her for a hundred dollars, she'd say no problem. She made that in a week! But the day Cousin Ginny pinned her own address to the collar of Alice's coat, Alice took to the streets for good and never had nothing to do with Ginny again.

It took us three days to get to Beverly Hills on foot. Most of the time, there wasn't even a sidewalk, like they weren't expecting us. I kept looking for the Bullwinkle statue. So far all we had seen was three supermarkets, and some strange bushes. These people cut their bushes into the shape of cork screws and spiders. Why? It got Alice very nervous. Finally, she attacked some sharp-edged shrubs that were coming at us from a pink-on-pink house. I think the hedge got the worst of it, but Alice took some scratches and we had to get some medical help at a gas station.

The gas station man wouldn't let us use the bathroom if we didn't get gas and we didn't have a car. I told them we did have a car, it was waiting for us at the best hotel in town where the moonlight twinkles on the water. I really *felt* what I was saying, you know. Then I told him about my telephone mistake and about my clock and my camera and my wallet. I asked him if he smelled fruit punch like I did. I think what I really needed to do was talk to somebody. After spending a lot of time with Alice, believe me that happens. Loneliness takes you over like the flu. I told him that too. He says, "Listen, buddy, you better get goin' where you gotta go." I says, "You listen, buddy, sonny, mister, whatever you call yourself, I gotta go to the bathroom!" Push came to shove and I guess I got the best of it be-cause before you know it, we were in a patrol car driving much faster than we could have walked. I had to say, slow down, we're missing everything!

Soon we were back at the Best Western. We had

to start out all over again. I said, "Alice, so help me, you better keep your hands off the shrubs this time. Look at those scratches all over you."

I had to clean Alice up before we could head out again.

Now it only took us two days to get to Beverly Hills because we had some experience. What a place! There were as many dresses in the windows as Alice had on. I wanted to get something to eat but what money we had from the contest we already spent on jay-walking tickets. I couldn't get Alice to let go of that lunch money, either. You probably don't think it's worth much, but all of those coins are silver! I'm telling you, Alice is a frustrating experience.

Well, we bought a star map and headed up to the hills where all the houses of the stars are. It was still hot. And Alice started to wheeze. I said, "Take off one of your dresses, Alice." But she don't want to do it. I said, "Listen!" Well, she knows when I mean business. She took off one dress, red white and blue. She left it hanging on a bush the shape of a coat rack. "I'm coming back for that," she said.

*   *   *

144

Well, it was hot and my parka was dragging. I brought it along just in case. You've got to have something to fall back on, you know.

The hills were so steep and we could barely get up there. Many of the neighbors were out in their yards raking and trimming and mowing, but they didn't respond to us, or to our pleas for water.

Just when I thought all was lost, another patrol car pulled up to help us. The officer asked for our identification. I said, "I'm Lew! This is Alice!" He said, "No, I mean in your wallet!" He was a big man, about eight feet tall. Even with the heat his clothes were dry and crisp. I bet you could bounce a quarter off his chest. I said, "You should be very proud of yourself. You look great. Don't ever be ashamed of who you are."

He said, "Your wallet, sir!"

Maybe it was the word *sir* that shook me up, or just the way he said it. Business. It got me so riled I didn't know what I was saying. "Oh," I said, "I lost my wallet. I do have a picture of it right here in my pocket, though, I think. Where is that . . . I lost my camera too but that was impossible to take a picture of. Hey, did you ever feed a robin and watch it fly away with a belly full of your good intentions? Makes you feel powerful. Can you tell me where

Bullwinkle is? And Sonny and Cher. Where do they live?"

Alice got scared. She got so unglued she started to peel off another dress.

So he drove us to the police station. I thought he had recovered my wallet the way we were driving. On the way there, I saw many of the sights I wanted to see, but they were whizzing by so fast I could hardly remember it. "Slow down, buddy! You're driving like a fool! Hey wait a minute, isn't that the Beverly Hillybilly House? Wait! Was that Disneyland?!?"

Wait! It was Tinkerbell circling above us! She was just about to sprinkle us with stars when she got too close to the windshield and was smashed like a mosquito. The policeman sprayed her with fluid, and turned his wipers on! It was a terrible sight. Alice started bawling like a baby and I wasn't too far behind. This maniac would have run down Goofy if he had the chance. No respect for human life whatsoever!

The contest people came for us at the station to drive us back to the hotel. They were steamin' mad but Alice made them go back for her dress anyway. It was still hanging there, blowing in the wind like a flag. Her own flag. It choked me up pretty good. It made me feel that special feeling I had for Alice deep down.

That night I sat up in the contest car until very late, rocking myself to sleep in the automatic adjustable seat, singing myself a little song. Times like this you wish you had a teddy bear.

When I woke up, I was in my own bed. At home! My alarm clock was ringing. I tried to answer it because I thought it was the telephone. I picked up my clock and said, Hello? Hello? But it wasn't the phone or the alarm clock ringing. Maybe it was the doorbell. I said, Who is it? Who's there?

Sleep makes a fool out of you. Every time I go to sleep at night I feel like I won't ever wake up. That's why it always scared me when I was little and why my mother kept a nightlight on in my room all night long. Popeye the Sailor Man.

I sat up in my bed. I felt hot. I had my parka on, and my sox.

After a few minutes I realized I was dreaming. We didn't go to California. I ran to my window. Look, it's still here! I'm alive!

It was a beautiful sunny day. Picture perfect. I ripped off my parka and got dressed. I was going to go *out* for coffee this morning. After all, this called for a celebration, this is life! You gotta live life when you can 'cause it don't happen every day.

Then the phone rang. It was the contest man to tell me I was not eligible. He said, "You live in Chicago, and this is New Jersey. We don't know how you got our number, but . . . I'm sorry you don't qualify."

"Not as sorry as I am for you," I said.

Then I hung up.

I walked at a pretty good clip all the way to the Busy Fly. All the familiar faces were there. Vic and Carol, my cousin Joe, Ralph, Pete, Lucky, and Lucille. Just as I was sinking my teeth into a cherry Danish I saw Alice outside. She pressed her face into the window-pane 'til she turned into Joe Palooka. But I was glad to see her, can you imagine?

I brought her out a Styrofoam cup of strong tea and a powdered doughnut, her favorite, even though it wreaks havoc all around her. I wanted to tell her about the contest, the trip to Hollywood we didn't take, and my dream. But why bother? She wouldn't get it. Look at her face, all powdery from that doughnut already.

Joe come out of the Fly with his push broom, said good-bye to me and mumbled something about the nut house for Alice. But Alice, she don't need a nut house. Not as long as she stays in her own backyard where I can keep an eye on. Of the two of us, since we were kids, I'm the one who had the dreams, you know. She don't know anything about it. Alice can't ever dream, because she's got no grip on reality.

IN THE BELLY OF THE WHALE: LEN TUKWILLA DRIFTS TOWARD LOIS GANDY STOOTE

*I*t wasn't long ago that I fell in love with Wanda Pulisch. And it was my meeting with Wanda Pulisch that led me to Lois Gandy Stoote, the renowned sea-shell artist from Lost Horizon, New Jersey.

I met Wanda on a long bus ride from Bothell, Washington, to SeaTac Airport in Tacoma, where I was headed for lunch at the Tomahawk Restaurant in the United Airlines terminal. The trip from Bothell to SeaTac is not that far, but it is a long ways by bus, about six hours, and feels like six days. That's

151

Len Tukwilla talks about his life as a driftwood artist on a cable talk show.

how Wanda and I were able to fall in love. We were able to take our time.

The chili at the Tomahawk is mild and the corn bread is dry, but the view is very good—huge noses of the jetliners press against the floor-to-ceiling windows, breathing a soft, foggy mist over the glass. After they catch their breath, they're off to exotic places unknown. The pegboard may say Minnesota or San Francisco or Dallas or Spokane, but don't let that fool you. What is truly exotic is all the sky in between, being above it all—the shattered peak of Mount Saint Helens, the Rocky Mountains, the pink surface of New Mexico, or just the undulating puffs of clouds. That's when the flyer gets communion.

It doesn't bother me that I am only going to the Tomahawk Restaurant and that I never leave the terminal. I've never flown. I'm terrified of flying and obsessed with air-traffic control.

Wanda boarded the bus with me in Bothell carrying a plastic sack from the Wig Wam. (The Pacific Northwest is rich in Native American culture.) I boarded with my burlap sack filled with driftwood pieces, including some fine wormwood specimens. Usually, after my chili and corn bread, I sit and work the wood where I can keep my eye on the jumbo jets, the wide-bellied whales that inspire me so.

Every piece of art created offers a bird's-eye view into the heart of the maker, which is why most of my driftwood pieces turn out to be birds: eagles, egrets, cranes, sparrows, swallows, wrens. If a piece does not inspire a bird, it may inspire a whale or a turtle or a boat. Oftentimes the driftwood pieces are knotted twisty shapes, otherwise known as abstract art.

A piece of driftwood takes a long time to develop into art. It must be cleaned and worked with tools the artist must master. Contrary to public opinion, a driftwood piece doesn't happen overnight, unless of course you work on it all night long. When you start working on the wood, it is rough and dirty and is of a light color. It must be rubbed until it is smooth and polished until it is dark. After several hours of work, depending on the size of the wood, it becomes smooth and dark.

Now the artist must decide whether the piece is abstract or representational. Will it serve as a doorknob on a picket fence? A headboard? Usually the piece will speak to you immediately, the first time you spot it. Look for signs. If any part of the wood is jutting out, I usually think of working it into the form of a wing, thus a bird. Is the wood shape bushy or curly? If so, you may have a squirrel on your hands. Oftentimes a long smooth shape is a whale, which can be mounted on a knotted twisty shape which would then become waves. This is where you combine the abstract with the tangible. This is where the soul of the artist takes shape.

On my bus trip from Bothell to SeaTac, I told all of these things to the wide-eyed Wanda. I had her eating out of the palm of my heart.

Wanda came from Blurb City, Washington, a tiny, dry town in the southeastern corner of the state. "I came here for the rain," she told me. She was living now on Orcas Island and working at a bed-and-breakfast farm.

"Actually I got on the bus in Edmonds," she said, "but I got off at the Wig Wam to pick up some things. I have a keen interest in Native American culture. Actually, I'm sort of a collector."

"What did you find at the Wig Wam?" I asked.

"Oh, a totem pole pencil case and some Kleenex. I'm going to a funeral."

"I'm sorry."

"I haven't been out of the state in years, unless you count taking the ferry to Orcas. Honestly, nothing much of any distinction happened in my life until I moved there," she said.

"And what was that?" I asked.

"I was stung by three different bees in one afternoon. Can you imagine that? I had never been stung before."

"It's a good thing you didn't die," I said.

"No, I didn't. But my aunt did. I'm going to her funeral in Lost Horizon, New Jersey."

The name stung me like a bee.

"Have you ever had chili and corn bread at the Tomahawk Restaurant?" I asked Wanda.

"No, but I'd be willing to try it. The combination of Native American culture and Tex Mex might be worth investigation."

It was at that moment that I fell in love with Wanda Pulisch, and that I decided I would one day immortalize her in driftwood.

Wanda and I sat close together under a steady pelting of eternal Pacific Northwest rain. The bus was rolling, but I felt like we were drifting, across some watery wilderness off the Puget Sound, huddled together on a long smooth whale of driftwood from the mysterious forest in the sea.

I did not know that my chance and fateful meeting with Wanda would lead me to Lois Gandy Stoote. In the underground world of art, of which I am a member, Lois is highly regarded. A mysterious artist who refused to call herself an artist or sell any of her massive quantity of works, Lois was a heroine, an art-for-art's-sake artist, an angel.

An historic meeting between Lois and her famed brother, artist Edgar Stoote, was photographed by the famous Lawrence Luxembourge of Vienna. I had seen the exhibit in Seattle. It had turned all the underground art world's attention upon Lois. Part of the haunting display showed the legless Edgar, who had fashioned himself into a human tombstone and planted his abstract figure stoically over the grave of his father, Garfield Stoote. Lois arrived every day with a dozen white seagulls and a dozen white roses which she arranged at Edgar's feet, so to speak. The two never spoke, and the photographic essay was entitled "Sibling Gravery."

Lois continued meanwhile with her seashell art at the beach and with a performance art piece which only the sea gulls were allowed to attend. It was, however, secretly photographed by Luxembourge, at which time the entire art world was turned on by Lois's wild abandon.

Daunted by Lois's newfound fame, Edgar became a movable cemetery artist, fashioning himself into an Angel of Death, a civil war cannon, and a mausoleum. His work, however, came to a halt on

Halloween, when he claimed to have been shoved and pushed over by a witch and a hobo.

I wasn't thinking any of this as Wanda and I drifted in our mysterious wilderness. These thoughts came to me later, after I catapulted through exotic airspace, on my way to Lost Horizon, New Jersey.

Let me tell you the story I told Wanda on our bus trip from Bothell.

Years ago, while hiking out on the Olympic Peninsula, I found my first piece of driftwood. Or it found me. It was about three feet around and shaped like an octopus and was sitting amidst a gathering of bright wet ferns. I managed to wrestle the piece from its position and set it atop a pile of dead tree trunks. Then it began to look like a chandelier.

The discovery of the octopus chandelier shed light on my entire being, on my existential existence, if you will. Because when I moved it, it said something to me. Unfortunately not in English. But it sounded important. I stood close to it and listened some more. It was going on and on. I've always regretted not having a second or third language but never more than this moment.

I decided to carry the piece home with me and try to find an interpreter. The Bothell Senior Center provided me with an elderly woman who spoke in tongues, but removed from it's rain forest–like habitat and imprisoned in my woodshed, the ominous wood piece no longer communed with either of us. In any tongue.

I kept the piece hanging to dry above my woodburning stove. Each morning I went out to my shed and sat beneath my prey, contemplating its lost powers, and feeling inklings of my own. Then I took it down, rubbed it, polished it, and I hung it back up. Like a dead deer.

"You must understand," I told the driftwood. "You're a found object now. A piece of art. A discovery. You are many layered. I have transformed you." I have transformed myself, I said, not aloud. For it was not until this moment, or perhaps the moment that I had found the piece of wood, that my life had truly begun.

The giant mahogany-like piece hung in a silent, wordless agony. Then, without warning, it stretched out its giant claws and moaned, and rain began to spray against the window. When I went to close it, I noticed the most fascinating and wondrous thing: My yard had transformed itself into a rain forest! Giant fern sprouted up from thick black soil. Long stems of iridescent green leaves dripped from a ceiling of thick dark evergreen and massive varieties of foliage. I heard deer calling to each other and an orchestra of piano and harpsichord. Streaks of orange sunlight shone through the slits in the trees, and a blue-yellow gaseous rainbow spun out of a lily-padded pond.

I pulled away from the window and fell to my knees. I did not know who God was, but I knew where he was, and I crossed myself. (I don't know why, I'm not Catholic.) But that was how I found my calling.

The rain forest lasted only a few moments, I guess. When I looked again it was over. The problem with something like this is that after it's over, you expect it to happen again. But it didn't.

I kept collecting driftwood pieces, and making driftwood art. My life became my creations, and when I did not create I had no life. No God. I started a little gallery and I sold much of my work. But my masterpiece I left hanging above my wood-burning stove, untouched and not for sale, though there were many offers.

Then one winter I went out to the shed and found my calling, my dream, in black cinders in a neat pointed pile on the floor. Somehow, a spark from the stove had gotten to it, and burned it. I never heard so much as a cry for help. If you're a driftwood artist, I don't advise you to keep anything near a stove, as it might meet the same fate and thus give an anticlimactic end to your story, or to your life.

I told this story I'm telling you to Wanda. When I finished she said, "Len Tukwilla, come with me to Lost Horizon. Come and meet my Aunt Lois. She's dead, but she'll know what you're talking about."

And so, after a bowl of mild chili and a piece of dry corn bread, I walked through the long, carpeted umbilical cord with Wanda Pulisch. It led us into a mouth in the side of a jumbo jet, and directly inside the belly of the whale.

Once in the door, a woman in a navy uniform greeted us. She sounded like a parakeet. To the left of the entrance was a small door leading to the pilots. I reached into my burlap sack, and stepped into the cockpit.

"At ease, gentlemen," I heard myself announce. "I'd like to offer you a small token of my deepest admiration and driftwood. A small measure of my due respect for what you do and do so well. Can I get anyone a coffee?"

Everything was blurry. I didn't know where I was. I was really clammy. I'd never been on a plane, had never flown before, never wanted to. I'm a romantic about flying, but the hideous tales from the survivors of air wrecks haunt me for weeks after I read them. And I read them over and over. I can hear a woman's voice whisper in my ear, "I've flown all around the world, for years and years, and I've never had a problem." Moments later she's a fire-ball spiraling across a cornfield.

I pulled out the token of my affection from the burlap sack, a beautifully knotted shape of drift-wood entitled *Startled Squirrel,* and handed it to the pilot closest to me. All holy hell broke loose! Some-one tackled me from behind, and before I knew it I was handcuffed and on my stomach in the food service kitchen. Apparently my startled squirrel looked like a Luger. Not to me. To me it never looked like anything but a squirrel in the state of extreme surprise. But it's all in the eye of the be-holder, I guess. You see what you want to see.

It took two hours before everything was straight-ened out, in which time I was severely reprimanded, stripped of my driftwood, and disgraced (they called my parents). When I finally got to my seat, well, I was the most unpopular person on the plane. Except for with Wanda, whose patient eyes were filled with tears of understanding. It so melted my frozen veins that I pushed the call button and tried to order two cups of herbal tea and a basket of scones. You'd have thought I had asked for the moon!

A driftwood artist must have the patience of Job. When I made the decision to take my life into my own hands, so to speak, I knew that at times it might be a tedious venture. And, apparently, a dangerous one. There would be loneliness, long walks on dry-bottom lakes waiting for the right piece of wood to call to me, and the expense of tools. The thing is, after my initial spiritual experience with the octopus chandelier, a piece of dead wood never spoke to me again. (Although every piece of dead wood has a story.) I have since studied Italian, German, French, and Latin, so as to prepare myself for another encounter, but my yard has since remained just a yard.

These thoughts rolled through my mind as we moved toward the runway. I was strapped into my seat so tightly the whole bottom half of me was cold and numb. Wanda reached for my hand and squeezed it, a gesture which made me cry out in pain. No one of authority dared to check on us lest we be held up any longer.

Finally, we had taxied into position. The whale wet its lips, then whined, then shook violently as it catapulted down the runway. With one great surge we were thrust up into a layer of mist, and soon wrapped inside a cocoon of white cotton candy. In a few minutes we broke free, off into the wild blue yonder, and everything changed. I loosened my strap, my feeling came back, and before long we were offered refreshments from a serving cart.

For most of our trip we floated atop various shapes of puffed clouds, giving me much inspiration. As it got darker a golden moon appeared and I vowed to seek out that piece of driftwood that would tell the world what that moon had told me. A wave of driftwood-longing washed over me, and I once again pressed my call button. As it turned out, my driftwood sack had been stowed on board in an overhead compartment and would be given back to me when we deplaned. I felt contentment once again. Up here, communing with the new horizon inside of me, I was reborn.

Yahoo, I said to myself.

By the time we reached Lost Horizon, New Jersey, the moon was at midnight and flooded the beach in blueness. Waves pushed and pulled rhythmically, and we stood a moment to look at Lois's house. It was spectacularly still, rimmed in grief-stricken seashell owls.

We built a bonfire, and I burned a driftwood piece in a symbolic gesture whose meaning I did not understand and later regretted. (It was a perfect tugboat shape.) We talked of marshmallows and hot chocolate and weenies, and then, since we had none of these, decided to go inside.

It was indeed a melancholy scene. The egret on the doorknob drooped its head, and the shells that hung on long stretches of string did not tinkle when we opened the door. But inside, life was still everywhere. Hundreds of owls eyed us suspiciously, each in its own unique seashell shape. There were shell boxes, shell lamps, shell night-lights, shell ashtrays, shell coasters.

"My aunt had a one-track mind," said Wanda.

"Some of us have to have a one-track mind, Wanda, or else we'll derail completely and fall off into nothingness." Wanda seemed not to understand. The concept of somethingness and nothingness is understood only by those who have teetered on the brink of meaninglessness.

So, here were the inside workings of Lois Stoote, the subject of the photographs that had so haunted and inspired me. Just as I had the thought, I saw an intricate, tiny pair of seashell heels set next to a night-light on the floor. The room was illuminated by moonlight, and more and more objects began to appear. A seashell piano, a television rimmed in a round snail-like shell, a hat rack studded with horseshoe crab helmets, and an incredible portrait of a man, a twinkling mosaic made of thousands of pieces of shattered shells.

"That's my grandfather," said Wanda.

Above the doorway, a giant wood-and-shell eagle was swooping down, and one of its claws grabbed on to my shoulder.

"Yipes!" I exclaimed.

"Fido, cut that out," a scratchy voice from nowhere said.

"Wanda!" I cried out in a panic. "Wanda, where are you!"

"I'm right here . . . Oh, my. Look."

There, sitting atop a book shelf, was a tiny woman, about two inches tall and covered in minute shells.

"Aunt Lois?"

"You must be Wanda," the woman said.

The voice materialized in the shape of a woman, ghost white and in white silk pajamas. It sat down at the seashell piano and played "Chopsticks."

"All of this, all of this . . . stuff. This is not art. It's just an expression of loss and grief. It's just ritual atonement."

Wanda and I were speechless.

"Get me a martini, why don't ya? I'll show you my inner workings. Get me an ice cold martini, straight up, with a big fat anchovy olive sittin' at the bottom of the glass, soaking up the ambiance. That's what inspires me. Why don't you figure out how to mix me up one of those, huh?"

"Now, Aunt Lois, I'm afraid I don't approve," Wanda said solemnly.

"When did the concept of approval enter into the sea of life?" asked Lois. "I wish I understood that. I never hurt a flea, or I never meant to. But I suffered. I never asked for friends or visitors. I made all this stuff as sort of a filler, filling in life, like solitaire. It just gave me a reason to walk on the beach. It just gave me something to look for, for Christ's sake. I never wanted it to amount to anything."

The white iridescent woman faded away, and we were once again talking to the tiny shell lady.

"Isn't this pathetic?" she said. "I've come back as a knickknack. Boy, I hope Edgar doesn't find me. He'd sure make a freak show out of this."

"Lois," I heard myself say, "why don't you come back to Bothell with us?"

"What the hell is Bothell?"

"It's where I live. The Pacific Northwest. It's a

nice town, near Seattle. And we have a very active senior center."

"Who said I need a Senior Center!" Lois bellowed. "I'm a loner, a staunch individualist, a unique spiritualist, I'm artistic—"

"Ha!" said Wanda. "You *are* an artist."

"I said artistic. There's a big difference."

"Will you come back with us?" said Wanda. "My dad will just take this place over, you know that, and turn it into some sort of salon or a museum."

"Don't you get a lot of rain out there?"

"Yes," I had to admit.

"And isn't there a high suicide rate?" she asked.

"Oh, who cares," said Wanda. "You're already dead."

There is a piece of driftwood sculpture that sits atop my mantle. I call it *Swirling Clouds.* Yes, it's close to a fire, but isn't life about taking risks? Instead of a bird perched rather predictably on my cloud, I placed Little Lois. Since her arrival, she has been strangely quiet, but we notice that she occasionally lifts her skirt to reveal a terrific shell-studded leg, which she crosses seductively over the richly grained wood.

I married Wanda Pulisch. She has transformed our yard into a lush garden, filled with found objects, mostly from the Wig Wam. I continue my life as a driftwood hunter, searching dry lake bottoms, gullies, and roadsides, looking for the moon, looking for the meaningful bits of abstraction. Looking, looking, looking. And listening. All dead wood has a story to tell.

JUNES, GIRLS, AND CIGARETTES

I come from a family of six kids. My father was a writer and a musician. My mother was a nurse and the kind of mother who made dolls out of clothespins and dolls' cradles out of tomato crates. Except for my oldest brother and sister, none of us were spaced more than two years apart, and we made up almost all of our own games.

My oldest brother Mike often played alone. He made a basketball game out of players he cut from sports magazines. He colored in their uniforms with magic markers. He made basketballs out of cigarette foil and gum wrappers and stored them in matchboxes. The back board and hoop were at-

tached to a stack of three books, and he sat at his desk every night, making that sound of the roar of the crowd.

Mike drove an arm chair with a pan lid, which we called a pan driver, and he made an altar on the back porch and said the Mass in Latin. We attended his Masses, received Wonder bread communion, and went to confession behind sheets he hung on a line across the wall. He also used sheets for his vestments.

My brothers Brian and Kevin made bolo balls out of my mother's nylon stockings, which they stuffed with other stockings and socks or something—I never had the courage to find out. I also never had the courage to really play bolo ball with them, as it required getting beaned in the head, hard, and laughing about it.

My sisters and I played Junes, in which all of our names were June and we sat around with coffee cups and paper cigarettes talking about our lives as housewives. Our husbands were always a very abstract part of our fantasy.

We played Girls, cutting out the heads of girl catalogue models, separating them into cliques, classrooms, volleyball teams, cheerleaders, and dorks. We colored some of the skins brown to make blacks, and inked in some of the hair very dark to make Puerto Ricans, neither of which were yet in evidence in catalogues. Every head had a name, a personality, and a history.

We made cut-outs who had extensive wardrobes, miniature books, and miniature wallets with tiny pictures we cut from magazines, and we made doll houses out of shoe boxes.

We all had characters we played, and now that I recall them I guess we were begging to be analyzed. My sister Cathy had a character simply known as the Rich Girl who would emerge from the fireplace and call us names, like Dirty Poorsies. We would then defend ourselves vehemently until she crawled back into the fireplace, and later we would discuss how we had really fixed *her*.

I became an entire family of bears who lived in the back of my brother's closet. The most prominent bear was named Guilty Bear (we were Catholic). He had two brothers, one named Potato Bear and the other named Pancake. When I got tired of doing them, they moved to California.

My sister Mary had a character named Tiredseedious who said only, "I am so tired of this," and I had a character who said, "Me no-no drive no donkey," in a monotone singsongy Spanish accent.

I would repeat this over and over until someone hit me.

The one character who sustained herself was the extended personality of my doll Joann. She became a staple item amongst my friends. Throughout the years her voice lasted, and when I finally became a performer in 1981, she became a performance piece. I am so neurotic about Joann that she has never been on television, though she has been the last piece in every performance that I give on the stage. She has never aged past six, and when my father died, a young memory gave me a clue as to why. At that age his hand would fall next to my cheek and I could press it there. My size has never been more perfect.

My brothers and sisters, like all brothers and sisters, are bound by a common, exclusive language, I suppose. Whenever we get together we still tell all of our experiences in the form of stories and characters, which is why I miss being with them so much, and probably the reason I chose to do what I do. Although somewhere, I'm sure, there is another explanation.

—Nora Dunn

My brothers Brian and Kevin

June Rae Klotty:
I Am Surrounded by Idiots!

I got this coffee mug from the people at work. See what it says, I AM SURROUNDED BY IDIOTS. Exclamation mark. Couldn't be closer to the truth. The world is run by idiots. It's an idiot's delight. You remember that sundae don't you? Idiot's Delight. My son ordered one once. We told him he could have anything he wished for and he wished for the Idiot's Delight. It's got fifteen scoops of ice cream mixed with every kind of topping. But when you get it, you realize it's just all the off scoops. Peppermint, New York Cherry, Coffee, with coconut flakes and pineapple syrup. That kind of thing. I guess they just knew some idiot was going to order it and eventually some idiot did. I never gave my son that choice again. I said you blew it, buster, now you eat it.

Why are people idiots? Why do the idiots run the world? I mean, the President of the United States is an idiot's delight. Every scoop of that man is false. I can sit in my living room and see that. These men are never the flavor we ordered. I stopped ordering. I don't vote. Why should I make an idiot out of myself? Be one of the sheep? That's what I see when I look out my kitchen window, fake sheep grazing in my neighbor's yard. The idiot family.

They have surrounded themselves with patio garnish. Fake flamingos, fake frogs, a cluster of fake mushrooms reminds me of a relish tray and you don't know what you're getting when you get a relish tray it's for idiots. But they've got it. They've got a cardboard cow. They've got Snow White and *four* of the seven dwarfs. . . . Finally these idiots put a three-foot-high wishing well in the yard, doesn't go into the ground, it's not a *real* well. Maybe they thought some idiot would come by and drop some money in it. Didn't happen. Their son fell in it, got stuck, almost died. That's what happened. He was upside down, his feet dangling straight up in the air, looked like an idiot. I could hear his muffled screams. I did *not* call 911. Somebody else did. The firemen came, first one on the scene made it through the cluster of fake mushrooms only to trip on a wooden bee that says HI! Now is that any way to greet someone? Why can't you just say it yourself, why does a bee have to say it? It took the firemen six hours to pull the boy from a three-foot phony well. I watched the rescue from my kitchen. They saved him. Idiot. They took him out for ice cream after—just guess what he ordered.

Of course the taxpayer paid for the whole thing, just like we pay for everything in this town. Take the parade. We had to give the troops a parade. The town was teepeed in yellow ribbon, the idiots across the street had the Three Wise Men on their front lawn carrying tommy guns. Were they here to protect me or kill me? I never really knew who the Three Wise Men were, but now they're armed and they may be dangerous. Am I supposed to participate in all of this? Do I have to line up with the rest of the idiots? The sheep? People around here are still complaining that we didn't have a Vietnam parade. We lost! If you don't shoot the turkey at the turkey shoot you don't win a turkey! But at least that war had a name. Vietnam. This last one was called the Gulf Crisis, then they called it Desert Shield, then it became Desert Storm, now that I'm finally figuring out what it was really all about it has no name. No identity whatsoever. I don't know what to call it, maybe idiot's delight. Yes, let's have a parade. We killed one hundred thousand people, I guess we deserve one! Let's march!

My daughter was in a parade once, sixteen years ago, a baton twirler. Now why would anybody want to twirl a baton? Talk about spinning your wheels. I said don't do it, you are setting yourself up for failure and humiliation, there is only one thing that can happen and that is you will throw up that baton you will drop that baton and make an entire idiot of yourself your thighs cannot take that kind of exposure, but she did it. Dropped the baton, humiliated herself, blamed me for the entire rest of her life. Now that my daughter's grown up she tells me she had a painful childhood. All I hear about is her painful childhood. I said why are you telling me now? Why didn't you tell me when you were a child, when I could have done something about it? Idiot. Forget your painful childhood, focus on your painful adulthood. Think of your brother's childhood, it was much worse than yours. Thank God. But she doesn't believe in God. She doesn't understand Him.

Now I believe in God, but let's face it he has a dark side. He works in mysterious ways. Sometimes idiotic ways. But he's God. We don't *have* to understand him. She thought her father was God, so did I we both made a mistake. Mr. Masculinity couldn't even kill a mouse like a man. He was a complete and total idiot. He didn't even come close to being God. My daughter can't understand that. She thinks the man was a saint. She doesn't believe in God, but then she wants to throw a dime in that wishing well. Mother, let's go make a wish together. That wishing well is not a symbol of hope, it's a symbol of near fatal accidental death. And when I die I don't want to go by accident. Let death take me, I can take it. Any fool can be born. Any fool can have a child. Unless you're a man. Then you can pull a Houdini and disappear. When you're a mother, you cannot disappear. Believe me I have tried it cannot be done! My daughter thinks if she wishes hard enough Mr. Houdini-Disappearing-Act-Father will rise up out of that wishing well, walk in here and scramble her some eggs. And I'm going to brew the coffee! Now if that isn't the most idiotic wish in the world, then my guess is there is no world. And if there is no world, then where are we? I'm in my kitchen I don't know where anybody else is I don't care. Idiots . . .

CONVERSATIONS
WITH JOANN

I used to really love my teacher, Miss Stone. I looked forward to being in school because of her. She was the best teacher. She really, you know, loved us, I think. You got the feeling she cared about you. She took a personal interest. She was pretty happy, she had a lot of ideas. One time she brought someone to school in a big paper bag, and we had to ask it questions. It turned out to be Ben Franklin, sort of. Then one day she walked in the classroom late, first time ever, and she was just weird. Something wasn't right. She sat down at her desk, and she was, well, just on edge. She told us that we were all in the second grade together, except we'd be moving on and she wouldn't. She would be here forever. Forever! She picked up an eraser and threw it at Patrick Sullivan, and he wouldn't hurt a flea. Then she smoked a cigarette. Right in the classroom! She said, "That's right, kiddies, I smoke." She sat at her desk and she smoked the whole thing and then she smoked another one, and then she walked down the aisle and put the butt in Bea Feeley's inkwell. I finally realized she was stinkin' drunk. I said to Dave—he sits in front of me—I said, "Dave, should we get Walter?" Walter's the janitor. Whenever something goes wrong, Walter's the one you deal with.

Well, we went through a pretty weird day. Sometimes Miss Stone was happy and then she would just bottom out. She'd run into the cloakroom and stay in there for about half an hour. She stayed in there all through reading.

The next day our principal came in and said we would be getting a substitute because Miss Stone had become a substance abuser. (Not to mention the way she was treating us.) And she went to seek help at a substance farm.

So this substitute comes in and *she is old.* O–L–D. She can barely walk. The smallest steps you've ever seen. It's almost like she's skating but very slow and not on skates. Finally she sits down and everybody starts throwing things. We slammed our desktops up and down. She didn't do a thing. Nothing. How could she, at that age. She just sat there. Did you ever see a yogurt-covered raisin? That's what she looked like. Very, very wrinkly and white. She was a mass of age. She sat there for a while. Nothing . . .

Then she like whispered, "Do art . . . do art . . ." Do art? She didn't know anything. So we started up again, someone's lunch went flying across the room, a hard-boiled egg came out. That was a mess, but very funny. I think it was Dolan's. And then Lynna Ardilla puked. Just like that. The whole room just stopped. The substitute teacher, she does nothing of course. And Lynna, who I hate—I don't know why, I just hate her, I just do, everybody hates her— she acts like it didn't happen. She's ignoring it. Puke is dripping off her geography book! Onto the floor. And she's like, gone. Not there at all.

I said, "Lynna, this happened. This has happened. Face it!"

But she didn't even look at me. And I know how that goes. You're sitting there, everything is going well, you feel fine, and then, you puke. And part of you just leaves. But no one was doing anything. The whole classroom was stinking. We just sat there. Some people started laughing, so I said, "Dave, you better get Walter."

So Dave left and came back with Walter and Walter was mad. He had a big bag of sawdust and he starts throwing it all over Lynna. All over her! Walter said, "You kids are animals!" Then he left. And there was Lynna, sawdust sticking to her face.

Well, we returned to our workbooks. Things were getting back to normal. About ten minutes later I looked up at the teacher, and suddenly her head went down. WHAP! Like that. She was dead. Just like that. I guess it was bound to happen, but you know it takes you by surprise anyway. So . . . I sat in the front and could see her eyes. They looked like goldfish. I turned to Dave and said, "Dave, you better get Walter."

So Dave left. Walter came in, looked at the teacher, looked at us.

He said, "Who did this?"

Nobody, you know. Nobody did it. It just happened. Somebody yelled out, "Are you gonna use the sawdust?"

That did it. Now he was really mad. That got him. He lifted up this old teacher, behind her arms like, and he dragged her out, real fast. Fshshshshshshshshsh . . . one of her shoes came off, he just left it there. Poor Walter . . .

We sat in there for the longest time until finally Miss McGreedy came in.

"Boys and girls, resume your work," she said. "And try to act like human beings!" Then she left us there, with our workbooks, with that shoe on the floor. Nobody talked for the rest of the day. It was weird, how a shoe could be in charge.

I like to watch TV. I learn a lot. I still watch Mr. Rogers. I know people make fun of him. I'm aware of that. And I understand it, I do. But he's so . . . lonely. That's why I watch. I mean, your heart just goes out, you know. He . . . he has nothing. I mean, he comes home, he opens up that closet, there's nothing there. He only has one sweater and he has to tell the world. He makes such a big deal out of it, it's sad. And then he has to change his shoes. You know why? Because he has only two pairs. That's why he makes such a big deal out of that. He puts on these—I don't know what they are. They aren't like Nikes or Reeboks, they're not the good kind of gym shoes. They're black and they're flat on the bottom. No tread. That's why he walks that way, so carefully. He's not getting any suction.

And he has no real friends. Everyone who comes over is educational. They're there to teach and get out. And his house—barely a picture on the wall. I think the whole place is in black and white.

Not like Pee Wee's house. Pee Wee's got everything. His house is *alive!* You open that refrigerator, the food dances. He's got a chair that jumps every time you say the magic word. He's got a live head in a box with a turban on, a friend who's a cowboy, a bike that flies! I mean, you go to Mr. Rogers's, he's talking to the mailman and the mailman wants to leave, he wants out. Here's a grown man who really believes his neighborhood is that miniature town. He *really* thinks he came from there.

Mr. Rogers likes to go out to the kitchen. He says, "Let's go to the kitchen!" Oh, boy, I can't wait. I know there's nothing out there either. But he is truly excited about it. That's why you feel so sorry for him. You go out to his kitchen and he picks up a bowl of fruit, and he takes an orange in his hand, and he says, "This is an orange." I don't think he's aware of what's going on on other channels. I don't think he even has a TV. You can click away and come back later and he'll be peeling that orange. It's pathetic, but how can you turn your back on him?

After I watch Mr. Rogers, I like see the "Wild

Wild World of Animals." This is my favorite show.
Have you seen this show? It's not easy to watch. It's,
um . . . every time I watch it something gets eaten,
you know. It puts you on edge. There's a voice, a
calm voice, like Mr. Rogers's. It's in charge. And it's
looking down over everything. It's looking down on
a bunch of moose. The voice says,

> This is a herd of reindeer elk.
> They are running, running, running
> to get away from the long winter ahead.
> The herd is fast,
> but not every moose will make it.

As soon as this voice says this, sure enough one
of these moose slows down. Whatever this voice
says happens, believe me. So this moose starts
slowing down. He's got a leg problem and he starts
looking back and I'm saying, "Do not look back
now, fix it later, get going. Whatever it is, it's not
worth it!" And the voice says,

> In this terrain there are often wild bears,
> hungry bears, hunting for slow weak game.

Sure enough, as soon as he says this, a bear is
in the bushes. And, he sees this moose and he

looks at him for a while and I'm thinking, Why doesn't somebody stop this? *I* know what's going to happen. But the man is very calm, and he says,

The bear has spotted the moose.
He will be patient with his prey . . .

And then this bear takes off and you have never seen something going so fast and this moose sees this bear and he tries to run and he looks ahead but the other mooses are long gone. They are not waiting for him, they don't even know who he is. So the bear is catching up to the moose, and I'm thinking, do something! Do something! Throw down a big piece of meat or a tire or something, anything! I know somebody's up there, but they're not saying anything anymore. The voice is, like, out for a sandwich. The bear's got the moose by the antlers and the moose is kicking and his legs are flying up he's struggling struggling struggling he won't stop struggling. He must be pretty out of it. He should play dead and then when the bear stops to look, he should run away. But finally this moose is, well . . . he's very still.

    I . . . I don't feel happy. But I feel . . . relieved.

    And I just hate this bear. I do. From the bottom of my heart, I hate him. The bear looks around to see if anybody saw what he did. But nobody did. At least he doesn't get that satisfaction. He's proud of what he did!

The man's voice comes back, very calm,

The brown bear is proud of her conquest,
now she can feed her hungry cubs.

And then you see the cutest little cubs you have ever seen. And I remember that I love bears, I have a couple of bears myself, and for a minute I forget all about that moose.

The bear cubs come running over, and they gather around the moose, like a dinner table, and they eat the moose. Right on TV! And I remember this show I saw on nature where a moose jumped out of the forest and attacked a herd of sled dogs and killed every one of them. And I'm thinking, maybe this is the same moose. Maybe he got a dose of his own medicine. But I can't be sure . . .

Overall, the show makes me sick. But for some reason I keep watching.